"This book is a "MUST READ" for anyone directly involved with children. As the mother of four sons that have been the victims of sexual abuse, I recommend this book to all victims and their families."

ock, Ohio

"If you   tors, you
NEEL   er read."
                                           er victim

15
16

"My b   tation. I
highly   :one like
that ir

alifornia

"This   ok. His
voice   voice of
the se   d urgent
voice.

te Prison

"By fo   offenders
to th   r peni-
tenc   heir re-
entr   :nt for
dece   igilant.
Alto   ubject-
area

m and
'anada.

"Pro   al, the
solut

agazine

OVERCOMING SEXUAL TERRORISM

Town Hall Edition

With Questions for Group Discussion

OVERCOMING SEXUAL TERRORISM

How to Protect Your Children from Sexual Predators

Jake Goldenflame

iUniverse, Inc.

New York   Lincoln   Shanghai

OVERCOMING SEXUAL TERRORISM
How to Protect Your Children from Sexual Predators

iUniverse books may be ordered through booksellers or by contacting:

iUniverse
2021 Pine Lake Road, Suite 100
Lincoln, NE 68512
www.iuniverse.com
1-800-Authors (1-800-288-4677)

All profits from the sale of this book will go to the author's continuing charitable projects in the reduction of sexual abuse worldwide through public education, victim assistance, community crisis intervention and offender reform.

Cover photo by Doris M. Bleier

ISBN: 0-595-34210-8 (Pbk)
ISBN: 0-595-67075-X (Cloth)

Printed in the United States of America

Contents

INTRODUCTION:
From Panic to Power

Every parent's nightmare is the same: that some maniac is going to break into their home and carry their child away forever: the light of their life. This book was written to help prevent that from happening. It can't guarantee that it will do so completely: no book can do that. But it will give you forty steps that you can take, using no more than your personal computer and your telephone, to arm yourself lawfully—right in your own home—against the threat of child sex predators in your neighborhood tonight. Chapter-by-chapter, it will tell you how to guard your loved ones from:

- rapists and child molesters in the streets,
- on the Internet and
- in youth organizations;
- repeated sexual abuse,
- child prostitution,
- incest, and
- repeat sex offenders who move into your neighborhood.

By the time you finish reading its pages, instead of living in fear for your safety and that of your loved ones, you will know what you and your own neighbors can do to make certain that no sex offender who goes to prison gets out unless he or she has been given the necessary treatment to do so without threatening you.

You will be able to make certain that any sex offender who does get out stays out of trouble or is kept under the tightest possible surveillance by your police department until he or she either enters a maintenance program or returns to custody.

You will know how a sex offender is formed so that you may take steps to help prevent any child you know from growing up to become one.

You will know how sex offenders think and act so that you may keep your own children safe from any who approach them.

And you will know how most sex offenders can be reformed because that's the kind who is writing this book. I was sent to prison as a child molester and have been out for over a dozen years now, without having any further problems. Make no mistake about it: others could do so, too, but as this book will explain that's up to you, in large part, for we either are our brother's keeper or his next victim.

The time to begin deciding what you should do couldn't be more urgent, as ugly storm clouds are now gathering in some parts of the country that could spread elsewhere. As of this writing, over a quarter of the United States either already have or are about to adopt laws that will ban many lawfully-registered sex offenders from living or working in many parts of America's cities and rural towns. ("Laws tighten on sex offenders," by Richard Willing in USA TODAY, May 12, 2003) Under their terms, those who have already been punished will be left to scratch out a living as best they can on the edges of the cities or scattered across the countryside, where some have already begun to angrily brood. "It makes you want to re-offend," one convicted sex offender told the *Los Angeles Times*.

We'll get to all the details in a later chapter—which states, and under what terms. The purpose of bringing it to your attention here is to use it as a *snapshot* of where we are now with regard to sex offenders. After a quarter of a century of increased criminal penalties and greater public awareness, the only thing that some officials can find to do now is expel every convicted sex offender who has *obeyed* the law and registered their whereabouts with police. Nothing could be more dangerous as that could lead many offenders to simply stop registering and live among you in secret once again.

Whether such laws survive legal challenges or not—and lawsuits have already been filed in at least three of the thirteen states involved—they're important indicators of what a significant part of the people already feel, which is terror instead of courage. This makes it very likely that, even if these laws are struck down, others just as dangerous will replace them and be duplicated elsewhere.

It is the premise of this book that you and your neighbors could do much better by establishing a front-line defense yourselves, right in your own neighborhood, while leaving those who have earned their way back with the chance to continue doing so.

It is vital to the safety of your loved ones—your children—that you learn how to defend yourselves lawfully, for the authorities can no longer do the job alone, that's what these laws also tell us. Budgets are too tight and other responsibilities are too great. All they can do is ship the problem elsewhere for the next watch—make things hard for them in one state so they migrate to some other—and you can't afford to let them do that. They may land near a relative of yours in another part of the country where you or your children may visit. Either you and your friends circle the wagons and prepare to take power back or you're going to be left waiting for a rescue that may not arrive in time.

For sex offenders, even if banished, will always return. They're already doing so.

According to the United States Department of Justice, almost half of all rape defendants are released *prior* to trial. For those convicted, the average sentence is just under 14 years and then they come back. Those convicted of sexual assault serve between eight and nine years and then they return. Even sex offenders placed in mental hospitals get out. The U.S. Bureau of Justice Statistics reports that, on an average day, 60% of the 234,000 convicted sex offenders not in prison are under supervision in the community, maybe your own. (That figure has since become outdated: according to *U.S. Census Bureau, Statistical Abstract of the United States, 2000* there are now over 400,000 registered sex offenders in the United States and figures are growing equally as fast in other countries.)

What can you do to see to it that these people are adequately controlled instead of being wished away? How can you protect yourself and your family—your neighborhood—if you suddenly find that a convicted sex offender is living down the street from you tonight? As this book was being written, the United States Supreme Court approved publishing a list of every convicted sex offender in the country on the Internet, so you can learn who they are. But what can you lawfully do with that information that will make your life safer and protect your loved ones if a sex offender is living nearby? What can people in other countries do, under similar laws?

This book will supply some of the answers. Read and weigh what it says. If it rings true, accept it. If it doesn't, use your own answers or someone else's. But, whatever you do, be certain of what you rely on as the safety of your loved ones will depend upon it.

Other than those individuals listed in public records, all names used in this book are fictional so as to safeguard the privacy of the individuals involved. For this same reason, only analogies of actual sexual conduct have been presented and no graphic depiction of sex with children is included. Where anyone has been left out of this book's account it was only because no way could be found to refer to them without making their identity known, at least to some others, and I give myself no right to do that. They may be certain, however, that they will never be forgotten and that, through this telling, others will be spared their pain.

None of the several references that have been made to *The Oprah Winfrey Show* or Oprah herself are meant to imply any endorsement by them of this book, only the author's gratitude to them for having featured his work on one of their programs where several points were made that are repeated here because of their importance.

A number of people have helped in the creation of this book, ranging from former victims to former offenders, family members of both, members of the treatment community, law enforcement and community corrections. My gratitude goes to all of them for sharing their experience and knowledge, but I, alone, am responsible for how accurately I have told what they have taught me. May our journeys heal others.

San Francisco, California
Summer, 2003

Introduction to
the Town Hall Edition

Aside from some phrases that have been rewritten to make their concepts clearer, the core contents of this edition of *Overcoming Sexual Terrorism* are substantially the same as the original. However, its purpose now is not just to inform the reader but also to make our democracy stronger by including five questions at the end of each chapter for readers to ask themselves, alone or with others, to rise above the alarmism that, too often, has dominated public discussion regarding sex offenders.

There are no right or wrong answers to any of these questions. You are invited, instead, to find the answers that are right for you. As a result, this book can now also be used by community discussion groups and as required reading material in college-level courses on criminal justice, psychology, sociology and related fields.

To make it even more useful, a highly-detailed index has also been added, so that any topic covered by it can easily be found when needed, e.g. when another horrible sex crime is being reported by the media and you want to try and understand it better.

Regardless of how this book is now read, its final purpose remains that of providing readers with steps they can take to overcome the sexual terrorism of our times or, if they are an offender, of being assured that there really is a way back for those willing to earn it.

Spring, 2005

Chapter One

The Making of a Predator

I've never met a sex offender yet who told me that he chose to become a sex offender. I've walked the yard with them in prison and I've regularly received their letters since getting out, yet I don't know of one who could say, "Yes: I chose to become a Sex Offender. I remember the very moment."

More often what I hear is that it was more like being struck by lightening and then finding ourselves scarred afterwards: there's a moment when we are seized by something and from then on we become it. Without warning, we found ourselves facing a force we could not explain, a power that has shown up again and again throughout the centuries, from Luxor to Athens, from Rome to Cathay, from the Cape of South Africa to the cities of the Sahara, and every time it appears it leaves people like us changed. That power felt so demonic that, before I got help, I came to call it *Lucifer*, yet I was only thirteen years old when I fell into that part of myself...

It was late afternoon on a Southern California summer day and I had been at the beach at Malibu with *all* the other kids from school—meaning, of course, only the most socially-active ones. Amidst cooling breezes from the sea that tempered the sun's thermonuclear heat, we had spend the day diving through the waves, lying in the sun and sampling the first wines of sexual attraction. But at four o'clock that afternoon the breezes intensified, telling us, like a mother's call, that it was time to go home and we reluctantly gathered up our clothes to trudge back to the nearby highway.

The girls all had parents who drove down to pick them up, as did some of the boys, but the more adventurous of my male companions sought rides from strangers, by standing on the side of the highway and sticking out their thumbs. Billy G. was among them—the *alpha*-male of our class and the one to whom everybody else's biological compass always turned. When he suggested I hitchhike with him, my 'yes' was automatic.

It didn't take long for the two of us to get a ride. A swarthy-looking man, chunky and in his late thirties, quickly pulled his car over and leaned to open the door on the passenger side and we got in. "Whereya goin'?" he asked, as we adjusted ourselves next to him on the front seat. In unison, we replied, "West L.A.," and giggled to ourselves as the car drove off. Since Billy was going to be getting out first, he was sitting on the outside and I sat in the middle with my shirt unbuttoned over my bathing suit. When the man reached across me to press the door's lock shut, I noticed that he pressed the side of his hairy arm against my chest, as if trying to feel its adolescent smoothness. That seemed strange.

His conversation with us, however, was even stranger. All the way home, he talked of nothing but *sex*: how great it is, how much you can get, all the different kinds of things you can do with a girl. He spoke mechanically and stared straight ahead as he talked, as if in a trance. I thought that most of what he said sounded *dumb*.

My friend's stop came up first and he got out, leaving me alone with the man. My stop was another mile down the road and when we got there, instead of pulling over to let me out, he quickly turned right at the corner and drove a few hundred feet away from the traffic before he parked the car by the curb and turned off its motor.

He turned toward me and asked, "What's your name?"

"Robert," I replied nervously, for that's what I was called in those days.

He told me his. Then he said, "You know, all that 'stuff' you can do with girls you can also do with guys!"

I didn't understand, but he went on. "Look," he said, leaning toward me, "I don't mean to frighten you…but I'm a *homosexual*."

I froze in terror. Only recently had I asked my mother what that word meant and she'd said: "*a man who takes little boys up into the mountains, cuts them up and throws away all the pieces.*"

The word paralyzed me as a result. I was so frightened that I couldn't move a muscle.

The man leaned further toward me, then halted to look nervously from side to side, as if he was trying to see if anyone else was around. Something must have made him change his mind, for he suddenly moved back as he continued to speak.

"Y'know," he said, slumping back against his door panel now, "if you'd meet me here tonight, we could go over to my place and I'd give you a *real* good time. Whadaya say?"

A distant memory came forth, of my mother telling me: "*If you ever meet a crazy man, just say 'yes' to him and he won't hurt you.*"

"Sure," I replied. He smiled and all of a sudden I could move my body again. I would have said anything to get out of that car.

He suggested we meet at seven o'clock and I agreed, then got out to walk the rest of the way home. He started his car up again and pulled out in front of me. As he drove away, I noticed his license number and quickly memorized it *just in case he comes after me.*

The telephone was ringing as I came through the front door of my house. My parents weren't home yet, so I ran up the hall to answer it.

It was Billy. "Hey!" he asked. "How they hangin'?"

"Fine," I replied. He wanted to know if I was going to the movies that night, with everybody else.

I told him about the man who'd given us a ride and how he'd told me he was a *homosexual.*

"Weren't you scared?" Billy asked in awe.

"Nah," I lied. I told him how I'd gotten rid of the man by pretending to be willing to meet him later.

"Gee!" Billy said. He was impressed, and that made me feel important.

Twenty minutes later the phone rang again. This time it was Billy's *father.*

"Robert!" he announced. "Billy just told me what happened to you today. You were very lucky to get away from that man. He's a very dangerous person!"

I didn't want to talk about it with Billy's father. "Yessir," I said. But that wasn't to be the end of it, for he went on. "I've just spoken to a police officer I know and he's on his way over to see you."

Shit!

Two detectives arrived at my house from the Los Angeles Police Department. One said he was from "Juvenile" and the other from "Administrative *Vice*," whatever that was. In answer to their questions, I repeated what had happened that day and when I told them that I had agreed to meet the man back at the corner that evening at seven "just to get away from him," they glanced at each other.

The Juvenile officer spoke first. "Would you be willing to help us, so we can arrest him?"

Wow! A chance to help the police? I'd be a hero!

He said that all I'd have to do is go down to the corner to meet the man. His partner told me I wouldn't have to get in the car. "Just touch the door— we'll have squad cars hidden in the driveways, all up and down the street. The moment you put your hand on his window, we'll come get him!"

The other officer cautioned me sternly. "Just don't get in his car."

I was excited and went down there that night, as suggested, fifteen minutes before I was supposed to, just in case the man came by early.

As I stood there waiting, I watched as one group of cars after another pulled up to the traffic light at the corner and stopped when it turned red, waiting like a herd of cows until it changed.

After I had waited twenty minutes or so, I figured the man wasn't going to show up after all and I was ready to give up. But, just then, I heard a man call out my name from one of the cars stopped in front of me.

"*Robert?*"

I peered about, trying to find which one. He called my name out again and suddenly I spotted him.

It was my Uncle Lou!

"Robert!" he beckoned again, through his car's open window. "Get in and I'll give you a ride!"

I was scared-to-death that fifty police cars would suddenly surround him and take him away. Quickly, I looked aside and stood there without replying—trying to ignore him.

But he wouldn't be ignored. "Robert!" he demanded. "Get in!"

The light changed and the cars behind him suddenly began honking.

"Robert?" he called. The honking grew more insistent as I stared at a church across the street.

"I'm gonna tell your parents about this rudeness!" he yelled as he drove away.

I sighed with relief when he was gone.

A few more minutes passed. Then, several additional ones.

Finally, at 7:15, my efforts were rewarded. The man I'd been waiting for pulled up—right in front of me.

"Hop in, *Bobby*!"

I looked inside his car and saw him leering at me.

I stepped over and put my hand on the door—then dropped to the ground and quickly crawled back to the curb. A nearby bus bench was in sight and I got underneath it and curled up and closed my eyes. Before I knew it, police were everywhere and an older officer with gray hair came over and stooped down, like a reassuring grandfather. "You can come out now," he said, and helped me to my feet.

The detectives came over and said I had to go with them. "Down to the station."

"Why?" I had thought it was all over.

There were reports to do, one of them said. "We need you to tell the woman who types up our report everything that man said to you today."

Tell a *lady* officer all the dirty things that man had said?

They took me with them and she typed as they made me repeat *everything* he had said. I felt soiled by the experience afterwards.

When we were done, one of the detectives told me there wouldn't be a trial because the man was on *probation* from another county for doing the same thing. "We can just put him in jail there." Then he had another police officer drive me home and when we got there he spoke to my parents while I went to my room. They never mentioned the incident to me and I went back to school on Monday morning…

…where I was a *hero*! Billy G. had told everyone what I'd done because the police had told his father. And now all the other kids were looking at me with admiration. For the first time in my life, I felt like I was an *alpha-*male myself.

But that Friday night, one of the bigger boys in my school paired off with me as a whole group of us walked the streets of a nearby shopping area. When the others said they had to go home, he invited me to stay with him and soon we were walking by ourselves. As we came upon a two-story building still under construction, he urged me to go inside it with him, "Just to look around."

"Okay," I said, and followed him through the bare wooden framework of a doorway.

It was dark in there, but we could see well-enough from the nearby street lights. On the second floor, some rooms were already paneled with sheet rock and we went into one and crouched on the bare plywood floor, facing each other, to talk.

He asked me to tell him, in greater detail, what had happened between the man and me, and I repeated the story. At the end he looked over at me and asked, "Have you ever…?" naming various sexual acts.

I didn't know what one of them meant and he had to explain it to me.

"It feels neat," he volunteered, and within moments he had done several with me and taught me how to do them to him. For the balance of that school year we did the same, regularly. I never did learn who had taught him.

It ended as abruptly as it began. After walking up to him one day on the school yard to ask, as I had so many times now, whether he wanted to come over to my house 'after school again,'—which was our code way of saying *to have sex*—he responded sharply, "No! I'm not gonna do that anymore. That's what *queers* do!" and walked away.

I didn't know what he meant by the word "queers," and I didn't care. All I knew was that I *liked* what we had been doing and I didn't intend to stop. The truth, of course, was that I no longer could stop: I'd become habituated to it. Where he had suddenly found some inner wall that let him defend himself from urges that he did not feel were really his, I had nothing like that to resist the ones now breaking out within me, only the crumpled ruins of one that sat on an emotional *fault line* running back through all the generations of my family known to me.

Its Beginnings

The last time it became active that anyone can remember was in the 19th century, in a small peasant village in Russia, where my maternal ancestors lived. It was on a crisp spring morning after all the men had hiked down into the valley to tend the fields. Only the old, the women and the children were left behind, on a high plateau dotted with the wood and straw huts which served as their homes. Molly was one of the children, a little girl no more than five years old. She and her girlhood friend, Leah, were sitting on the ground, playing with stick-figures they had wrapped in scraps of cloth.

"Mine is the Czar!" Leah announced.

"Mine is his bride," replied Molly.

But the only marriage that day was to be with death, for as the children played, a troop of soldiers from the Czar's army came galloping up into the village—*to persecute the Jews for having killed Christ!*—and the village was suddenly besieged.

Women screamed and ran for their lives as huts were set aflame. Only the children failed to move, paralyzed by shock. As Molly and Leah sat mutely beholding the horror unfolding in front of them, a horse the color of midnight rode past as its rider leaned over and held his sword out like a scythe. Effortlessly, it harvested the tiny head of Molly's playmate, right in front of her.

Little Molly was found after the soldiers had left, still sitting mutely, directly across from her playmate's lifeless body, lying on its back in a pool of blood. A blanket was quickly thrown over the tiny corpse and relatives gathered up Molly and comforted her as best as they could as they carried her into their hut and placed her in bed. There was nothing else they could do and the child's life continued from there. Over the next dozen years, she grew up and her parents took her with them when they immigrated to the United States where she soon married a man from a similarly ill-starred family. Ultimately, she became my maternal grandmother and wore a permanently-tragic look which stamped itself on all of us who descended from her.

Or the story may actually have been about *her* grandmother, the family chronicles aren't clear. All I know for certain is that, somewhere back there, the wholeness of life was shattered for my family—like so many others in lands plagued by war and social strife, whose children will also grow up mad and become the madmen of their times.

Like those to come and those before, our family became filled with descendents afflicted by suicide, depression and anxiety. They became habituated to responding to life as if they were its victim. Being unconscious of this, I unknowingly adopted it as my own way of seeing myself. It became my *myth of self*: who I thought I was.

"You were raised to become a walking *time bomb*," my first prison counselor told me, looking over my file. "You could have gone off a number of different ways. It just *happened* that you became a sex offender."

My mother's childhood was an equally-shattered one. She only vaguely remembered her father, and then with great sadness. The *official* version in the family was that he fell down and *hit his head* in New York City after they had all come to America. But, whatever the actual facts, he wound up being committed to a mental hospital for *depression* when he and my mother and her mother reached California. My mother said that she never forgot taking the long trolley ride down to the city of Santa Ana from Los Angeles each weekend as a child, to visit him there.

"He had been such a *strong* man," she lamented. "It hurt *so much* to watch him wither away."

The *fault line* spread into her generation.

He died in that hospital when she was five years old. Left to be raised by grandparents while her mother went to work in an uncle's clothing store, she was given an often-insensitive upbringing. Her grandmother, while described as sweet, was also intimidated by her gruff fundamentalist husband, an Orthodox Jew who spent all day praying for God's favor with such fervor that one might wonder if he really trusted his Deity to know that he needed it.

One day, while still little, my mother fell down and broke her arm. It was a compound fracture and she recalled how she could clearly see its two shattered ends poking underneath her skin. In shock, she went home and entered her grandfather's study, mutely holding her arm like a broken wing.

In sharp response, he set his prayer book down angrily and rebuked her for interrupting him. "What's the matter with you?" he bellowed. "Can't you see that I am busy, *speaking to the Most High?*"

She was left an emotional pauper. Fearful of men, but always believing herself to need one, when she grew up she married a man who dominated her, probably in revenge for the way he recalled that his oldest sisters had brutally raised him.

The Flaws of Childhood

An inwardly timid man, he became a lawyer and sought refuge in the field of law hoping thereby, like most lawyers, to control life. Constantly assuring me that our existence was full of absolute rules, the main lesson he taught was that the only way we could keep from being crushed by the world was by somehow gaining support from its fundamentally-unsympathetic Judge.

Afraid of others wherever he went, he could not even find the confidence to cross the street if there was a car coming anywhere within eyeshot. Holding out his arms to restrain both my mother and me at the curb, he'd keep looking back and forth repeatedly while cautioning us, "Wait 'til it's past," even if it was a block away. He'd do the same and halt us, even if we were halfway across if he saw one coming, causing it to honk angrily at us to *get the hell out of the way!*

Yet, for all his timidity in the outside world, at home he was The Autocrat of the Dinner Table, insisting bombastically that dinner always be served promptly at 6 PM whether anyone was hungry or not. If, for any reason, the evening meal failed to arrive on time, he'd holler at my mother. *"What's the matter with you? Why isn't dinner ready?"*

Almost immediately, she'd hobble in to serve him, a hastily-filled plate in her hands. But, afterwards, she always let a vicious streak of backbiting break out in her as vengeance against anyone she lacked the courage to face directly. When I was just at the dawn of adolescence, she took me aside and told me in hushed tones that I was adopted because they couldn't have any children.

"*It was your father's fault,*" she whispered.

More seismic damage.

Starving for love, my father didn't know how to attract it, so he took it wherever he could. Every wedding anniversary and holiday, he bought my mother the most effusive greeting cards he could find, then read them aloud as he swooned to himself before clasping me to him and covering my face with thick, wet kisses. As she was frigid, I was made into her emotional surrogate.

She despised the human body and its sexual organs in particular. I still remember her scowl when she had bathed me and touched mine. Once— when I was no more than four years old—a hearty banana plant unexpectedly grew up in our Southern California front yard, where it promptly sprouted a large bud looking exactly like an uncircumcised penis. Immediately upon discovering it, my mother ordered the gardener to hack the offending member down.

Not long afterwards, I duly imitated her by plunging the third finger of my left hand in-between the moving blades of our gardener's lawn mower.

The severed member was sewn back on, but fears of adequate potency remain with me to this very day.

Like her mother before her, she was a chronic worrier, a perpetually shifting sea of self-doubt constantly flooding my island. Amidst such forceful tides, it was impossible for much of a self to congeal within me. Early in my childhood, her stare of disapproval at my very dancing to music on the radio even froze my body. Take a good look the next time any convicted sex offender is on the TV news and you'll see that same rigid look stamped all over his. Forbidden to physically express ourselves, we celebrate our bodies only in secret.

At seven years of age, the final ingredient was put into place to keep me off course for years: I began to shut off my feelings because my parents kept telling me that they weren't real. Every time that I said I liked something that they didn't like, they'd insist *"You don't really like that."* Similarly, whenever I had an opinion any different than theirs they insisted that it didn't matter.

And as a result, all the grounds were now there from which a sex offender (or almost any other kind of severely disturbed person) will grow. They aren't genetic: so far, the Human Genome Project hasn't had any success in finding genes associated with sexual offending. The sexual predator of tomorrow is still a child today, a very disturbed child. His or her care providers are usually insecure, alienated and plagued with emotional breakdowns in their own families of origin. The child's mother doubts herself and her womanhood, covertly was against her husband and overly-controls her own children. The father is emotionally distant, fearful and dictatorial in his home, unable to accept his wife as his equal.

The child is physically or emotionally abused and comes out insecure and unable to express his or her own feelings. Add *sexual urges* and such a person can become explosive, very possibly a future sex offender.

If you ever meet such a child, *befriend him* and you may save a life from turning in on itself and becoming destructive. If the child tells you that he or she has been physically or sexually abused, report it to police or Child Protective Services. If the child is being neglected, let the child know that he or she is welcome to visit you.

Saving the nation from its next serial killer, rapist or child molester is simple. If you meet a child who is hungry, feed them. If you meet a child who is cold, give them a blanket. If you meet a child who doesn't have a shelter, become one for them. Don't wait until they grow up to become every parent's worst nightmare. Dare to comfort them now and involve your neighbors so that the child has a small community of adult friends who can be turned to for help. It takes a family to grow a child. It takes a community to heal one.

An Incendiary Mixture

As soon as I entered my teens, even my sex life was dominated by my mother. Every morning after I'd been out on a date, she'd always interrogate me over breakfast for any of its erotic details and then applaud when I told her how I had gotten one girl after another to let me touch them in some forbidden place.

"Shame on you!" she would scold, with a sly wink of her eye as she stirred the scrambled eggs.

Buoyed by the early adolescent pride her responses gave me, I soon became even more sexually ambitious with my dates so I'd have more to brag about and, in the process, took on the mindset of a budding sexual predator.

But, at age 16, I found out how counterfeit my sexual feelings were when a classmate introduced me to a woman I could pay for sex downtown and I discovered that I couldn't complete the act until I began fantasizing about some of the secret practices in which I had now started practicing with some of the other boys in my school.

The result was even more stress, compounded by additional problems I was having at home with my father. I'd begun to read widely by now and realized that a lot of his ideas weren't the only ones after all. Yet, every time I tried to probe and question any of them, he would only explode in rage, angrily getting up from his side of the dinner table to rip his belt off and lash me with it as I cowered on the floor, covering my head in the corner in terror. By the time I graduated high school, I was so confused about myself and my life that I chose to enlist in the Army, to give myself more time to figure things out, before going off to college.

Looking back now as a convicted incest offender, seeking to understand how I became such a person, I can only quote the words of Sex Abuse Therapist Susan Forward, author of *TOXIC PARENTS*, "In some cases, the abused child unconsciously identifies with his abusive parents…as an unconscious defense, they develop some of the very personality traits (of) their toxic parent."

But I didn't understand that then, or myself at all, and when I later tried to get counseling about my sexual feelings in the Army I was threatened with a courts martial if I admitted to anything, so I returned at the end of my enlistment as confused as I'd been at its start. Within a week of beginning college, a sexual predator among the students on campus came after me and we began a relationship.

When Christmas vacation approached, he asked if I wanted to go to Tijuana with him, just across the Mexican border, where he said that we could have sex with boys there. I wasn't interested and he said that, if I needed any action while he was gone, there was a place just off-campus to which I could always go, one of the local bars.

"That place is *always* hot!" he volunteered, smiling wickedly.

I discovered he was right soon afterwards and began participating in anonymous homosexual couplings in its shadowy back rooms regularly. But at the start of the next semester this stopped when I met the first coed who really smiled at me. I was so anxious for the heterosexual life she offered—and all the comforting sense of normality that seemed to go with it—that she immediately became my only pursuit. By Easter vacation, we were lovers and, that fall, she was pregnant, we quickly married and my parents gave us money to get our own apartment.

My wife gave birth the following year and, as I held the baby in my arms at the hospital, I silently vowed to myself—in keeping with the homophobic views of those times—that I would never again commit another homosexual act because I wanted to be a good father.

I stuck with this resolve for several months but, under the strain of middle of the night feedings and a full load of classes, I soon found myself feeling depressed. In an attempt to get away from it all, I took the car one day and drove into Hollywood, to run some errands. As I waited for a traffic light to change, a theatrically-beautiful young boy who appeared to be in his mid-teens came over and asked for a ride. I said yes without even thinking and, after he got inside, I began talking to him about nothing but sex as we drove away: how great it is, how much you can get; all the different things you can do with a girl. I spoke mechanically and stared straight ahead as I talked, as if in a trance.

"You know," I said to him, as we waited for a light to change, "all that stuff you can do with girls you can also do with guys."

He was puzzled, so I offered him five dollars if he would let me have sex with him and he agreed.

I turned right at the next corner and took us up into the hills where I parked the car and we did it there.

Afterwards, I was filled with loathing toward him, as if it had been his fault instead of my own. I wouldn't even speak to him as we drove back down and, at the first corner we came to, I let him out and drove away. But, the moment he was gone, all my feelings of revulsion turned back on me and I felt sickened with myself for what I had done.

They didn't last. As I drove back home, replaying the whole episode in my mind, what I also remembered was how the whole thing had felt as if it had taken place in a *spell* of some sort. It was as if I had been *taken over* by something completely outside of myself the very moment I had encountered that boy—as if something had *possessed* me into seducing him!

Whatever it was, it took me out of this world with a euphoria that was absolutely intoxicating. I'd been as high as any narcotics addict. For just that brief period of time I'd escaped all the unresolved pains I still carried from childhood, and all the anxieties that were now their children. It was an escape too good not to seek again. By the time I got back to my apartment what I knew was that, if that seductive force ever beckoned to me again, I would *welcome* its embrace!

I was *Lucifer's* now.

*　　　　*　　　　*

Questions for Group Discussion

1. What warning signs could you see in a child who is on the road to becoming a disturbed person?
2. What could prevent this? How could the community, the schools, the child's neighbors intervene most effectively?
3. What can parents or family members do to make certain that their child's first sexual explorations are healthy ones?
4. We say that the child who is molested was a *victim*. Do they remain one if they go on to molest another child?
5. Even when they are an adult? And if not, why not? Where should the line be drawn between 'damage that has just passed on through them' to 'damage that they, alone, are responsible for having created'? Is there such a line?

Chapter Two

The Theology of Sexuality

Not all of us who are molested as children grow up to become child molesters. Most do not. As almost all of the experts agree, that only happens if the damage has been significant enough and we aren't given sufficient help afterwards. As I told Oprah, the damage doesn't have to be physical and she agreed with me: the damage is to the spirit. (*The Oprah Winfrey Show*, February 25, 2003)

There was a man and he didn't even touch me. All he did was offer to do so in a way that I found *extremely threatening* and damage occurred: as I said, I was so terrified that I couldn't move a muscle. That's a lot of trauma for a 13-year old boy to experience, to say nothing of the fright afterwards, from having to meet him again and then having to crawl into hiding until police came. Now add the humiliation that occurred, when I had to narrate every filthy thing he had said to me from the moment I first met him that day, and you have the total experience: terror, more terror and finally humiliation just when I'm about to start adolescence and learn what it is to give and receive affection from others outside of my family.

No wonder that my sexual expressions were affected. No wonder I was preyed upon further, by that bigger boy at school and then again, at college. There's a biological principle at work that we see in many species: when any member is wounded, the rest try and kill it off to keep the species as a whole strong, and that's what may have been enacted here.

Without help and healing, how does such a person survive? One does not. Instead, one chooses to give up their identity and imitate their attacker, perhaps so they will never be attacked again because they are the attacker now.

And, perhaps, also to re-experience the abuse in an attempt to figure it out by a mind left swamped by the sheer *mystery* of it all. Like the mythical *Persephone*, I was doing no more than trying to come home on a nice day when the ground suddenly opened up and a man carried me away with him. That event completely stripped away my assumption that I, alone, controlled my life. Who wouldn't be left trying to grasp at understanding it, so that it didn't happen again? The idea that we really don't control our own lives is as threatening as it is true.

So I went on to become a *victimizer* when that might have been prevented by an adequate counseling program. A seductive force broke out within me and from then on, like the *King of Hades*, it carried me off, again and again. I became a sexual predator: seeking young, teenage boys: seeking myself before I became what I'd become so that I could somehow understand it. One might as well try to see what the back of their head looks like without two mirrors to help them do so.

Treatment would have been better. If you ever have a child, or a relative who is a child, who has been sexually molested—or even seriously threatened with being sexually molested—use any of the national referral organizations for abused children listed under the Readers Resources section in the back of this book and take the child to a clinician. You may save a life from becoming dangerously warped.

And if you want the children who are abused to speak up and tell you, stop making it impossible for them to do so. It is the current fashion now to speak of the *pain* that a child molester brings: confusing the effect with the cause of his misdeeds. Child molestation leaves a lot of pain behind. I've met and worked with too many former victims to have any doubt about that.

But that's the effect, while the act of child molestation itself is rarely painful: it is a *sexual* encounter and involves nerve endings biologically programmed to experience pleasure by touch, whether the touch was that of a mother or a monster. And for the child who has experienced such a touch to admit it—in a climate where it's always spoken of as painful while the child remembers it as feeling *good*—is equivalent to asking the child to admit that they are a monster, too, and they are not going to do so. Like me, after I was first sexually used, they will be left in their own confusion as to how it can feel *good* when the whole world tells them that it is bad, *unless there is something wrong with them!*

What has to be done is tell children the truth: that a lot of things can feel good that are bad for you and the fact that they felt good doesn't mean there is anything wrong with you.

Searching the Night Seas for Sex

A short time later, out of college and now working, I had to drive through Hollywood to get home each day and in the late afternoons there were always a lot of teenage boys hitchhiking there. Intoxicated by my recollection of the incident with that first hitchhiking boy, seeing these others made me want to repeat it and I did so with them, whenever I could. As with that first boy, I offered them money for sex and they took it, for they worshipped money instead of self-respect.

Mind you, this wasn't because they were *poor* boys. My hunting areas never included the slums or economically depressed parts of town, as I knew that those were far too dangerous to enter. It worked, instead, because in the American culture we have this mindset that says 'money makes anything okay,' and they were the children of just such a mindset.

Not all of them, of course. I had my refusals. But I had more than my share of those who willingly sold themselves out for no more than the cost of a *Big Mac*.

I'm not saying it was the culture's fault or that of their parents. The fault for preying upon them was mine. All I'm saying is that this was where I found that so many were so very vulnerable: in their belief that money, alone, is all that matters when there are other values far greater. They just weren't being taught that any more. Not in our secular culture.

Having no way of knowing—when I stopped to pick up a boy— whether he would or wouldn't accept my proposition, I quickly noticed that a certain kind of boy was more likely to be susceptible than others: alienated boys, lost and outside of themselves, boys whose self-definition had not yet become set. Any boy with a strong faith in himself was never available to me, and since finding my kind required that I make an accurate assessment before I made my offer, I began psychologically-scanning every rider from the first moment that he got in my car.

I'd begin by asking him to tell me about himself, what he liked and what he didn't, whether he'd had any success with girls yet or not. What I did was ugly but, in his answers, what I listened for was any crack in his psychic shell through which I could insert a tentacle.

Lost as I was, it was impossible for me to think of them as my *victims*, or myself as their *predator*, for we didn't even have those terms then. Back in that much dimmer time, it only seemed like a harmless diversion on the way home, no more than a game that I was playing to amuse myself. I was so blind that I didn't even see it as cheating on my wife, *as no other woman was involved.*

People accuse us of being so deceptive: passing ourselves off like everyone else, just so that we can get close to our prey and strike. We're your banker or lawyer or service club president. We're your youth group sponsor. Man of the Year. Pillar of the church. Maybe even its priest.

But they don't know how deceptive we really are! The genius of our deception lies in the fact that we also deceive *ourselves*. We think that we're really *quite okay*, no different than anybody else, other than during these little *episodes* of ours. That's why we are able to deceive others. Like a spy posted to a foreign country, we pose as an ordinary person until we believe it, because facing the real truth about ourselves is so painful. The shame that hovers over us is like an impending avalanche. We fear that if we ever let ourselves see what we really are, so much shame will come crashing down that we will be buried under it, when the truth is that we're already buried under a power we know not how to conquer.

So we deny who we are to ourselves and, by so doing, deny who we are to you. Don't blame yourself if we succeed and your child is harmed. How could you have possibly spotted us when we also conceal ourselves to ourselves? Because I could not see how harmed I had now become through having been molested, how could I possibly understand that I was harming anyone else?

But, as time went on, I began to see something else that did trouble me: that the *urge* to go hunting for sex was coming upon me more often than before. All by itself it was beginning to increase in frequency until, finally, it was taking me over every ten days—and *making* me play whether I wanted to or not. That scared me, so I tried not to think about it. Every time the matter came up in my mind, I averted its gaze. But it waited for me—that sense of 'Other'—it waited in its own good time. A second self had now taken root within me: my urge for predatory sex had now become a personality as autonomous as my own. It had its own intentions and it didn't care at all about any of mine. It was my *Lucifer.*

His bouts always began the same way. I'd be living my life just like anyone else and then a pool of sadness would seep into my mind. It was like the moaning of an abandoned child and when that inner pain became too intense, I found myself suddenly thinking of *sex* with a boy in his teens! It always smothered that inner pain.

I wanted someone with a trim build and good, clean looks—still pretty-enough to be a woman. And if he was a little shy, or a little scared…*that was hot!*

I'd take my car and begin my prowl, and when I had someone who I thought might say yes, I'd bend our conversation to the subject of sex and casually ask if he had ever thought of experimenting with it "like some people do." It's the same thing that predators are doing on the Internet these days.

If my prospective victim said that had no appeal to him, I'd quickly agree—"I don't blame you; neither would I"—trying to seem just as normal as anyone else. I'd then quickly contrive some excuse to get rid of him so I could begin hunting for someone else. "Oh! I'm sorry. I forgot that I have to stop at a market up ahead. Let me drop you off here." ("Gotta leave the Chat Room now to go have dinner.")

But if he said that he was open to the idea, that's when the Mystery began to descend: that feeling of a *spell* invisibly being cast like a net over both of us, drawing us together toward something I couldn't name but which now commanded. Bewitched by the mood, I lost all sense of self and, instead, became just an urge. It became my exit strategy from a past full of hurt that still hadn't been healed.

A sex offender isn't that different from everybody else. He's just somebody who hasn't found any other way to announce that he hasn't been adequately loved either as he grew up.

Sometimes I didn't find the kind of prey I was looking for, only young men in campus restrooms or waiting on some secluded trail in certain public parks. They'd do in a pinch to satisfy my thirst. If the hour was late, I could always find a male prostitute on Hollywood Boulevard, but I really didn't care much for them as they had no innocence left to consume.

People sometimes ask me how many victims I had, as if that would tell them something significant. But I never kept score, so I don't know and I question whether the answer would mean that much, except to a clinician. I've known men who have had very few victims and then went on to kill them. I've also known others like myself, who had many, but finally stopped and remained free from re-offending for decades. In order to control sex offenders, what the public needs to understand is that, in every other way, we're just like anyone else. Just as a young, normal heterosexual male will have a certain number of successful sexual encounters if he has the looks or skill to attract them, so will a sex offender of the same age: the number won't be any more or any less. What's different about us is not how many times we do it, but who we go after, and why.

We seek alienated children, who aren't sure of themselves yet. If you want your child to be the kind we would never seek, just teach them this one thing from the very beginning: *"you can survive anything."* Tell them that enough and they will have the hard protective shell of self-confidence that gives them a suit of armor against people like us.

Like all serial offenders, I tried to resist my urges but repeatedly failed. They came when they would, like riptides, and whenever I tried to resist them, their current intensified even more.

Sometimes I'd believe that I could overcome them, if only I could find more *willpower*. Those were the times when I'd get close to that tenth day and let myself think: *this time I'm going to prevent it!*

It's over, I'd tell myself, and drive directly home without stopping to give anyone a ride. But my resolve was never strong-enough to hold and the next day the urge would return, even more powerfully: sex would be on my mind all-day and I'd barely make it home instead of turning off en-route to start hunting. Those were the times when I'd believe I had finally won. But, late that night, the urge would always return to evict me from my marital bed by a tossing and turning that wouldn't stop until I got out to slip my clothes back on and sneak outside while my wife slept.

'Just to take a drive,' I'd tell myself. 'Maybe go down to the beach and up the Pacific Coast Highway a bit. *Not for sex*—I don't want to do *that* again—but only to relax. I'm under a lot of stress.'

But instead of driving south, as I should have, if all I'd meant to do was go there, the moment I reached Hollywood Boulevard the tidal urge would swell within me and I'd swing the car into a right turn as I began trawling the night seas for sexual encounters. And as I trawled I'd begin to imagine what my ideal dream-boy would look like when I found him, until the picture of him that I formed in my mind became *so real* that I finally thought he really existed.

He'll be at the next traffic light, waiting for a ride!

And, when he wasn't there: *He'll be in Beverly Hills!*

He'll be down on the Coast Highway!

He'll be out in the Valley!

On through the midnight streets of the city I'd drive, chasing my phantom lover until dawn. Then I'd drive back home, exhausted, under the scolding light of a raw red sun—alibi-ing to my wife that I'd been out for a drive because *I hadn't been able to sleep last night.*

When my voyages were successful, I'd return from them as satisfied as the captain of a wealthy merchant ship. But, afterwards, I always had to face a band of angry harbormasters waiting within me.

There was the Unforgiving Customs Officer:

How could you have done this? It's 'sick,' All the psychiatric text-books say so. What's the matter with you? You're living like 'Jekyll-and-Hyde,' pretending to be so 'good' when, actually, you're just hidden evil!

There was the Master of the Brig:

You'll get caught, you know. It's only a matter of time. One of these days, the police are going to catch you, and when they do they'll put you away forever, like the madman you are!

And finally, the ship's insurance agent:

You'd better be sorry! You'd better get down on your hands and knees and beg for forgiveness, or those forces will carry you away forever and you'll lose everything!

Their roar was my own remorse and it always overcame me. *I'll never do it again,"* I'd promise myself. *"Never! It will never happen again. I swear it!"*

That would still them and then I could walk ashore. But inside myself I realized it would really take more than that; that what I really needed was professional help if I wanted to stay ashore. I was too frightened to get it, though.

They'd say I was 'crazy' and lock me up!

That's what I'd tell myself, but the truth was that I really didn't want help yet, for I still loved those voyages too much to give them up. Even though I realized I might get caught—and I was terrified at that idea—I couldn't stop myself. Their sheer dangerousness only heightened their intoxication. I came to *like* the zest that danger gave, so much that it didn't matter what the penalties might be. *They could pass all the laws they liked and it wouldn't have made any difference.* Laws are persuasive only to a rational man, not to one commanded by his urges. Or with a person who secretly wants to destroy himself. It takes *work* to run a life responsibly and, if you aren't adult-enough to accept that fact, the idea of letting it all get washed away can also sound *deliciously liberating*.

And so I continued to fall, thinking that, eventually, there'd be a day when I'd *outgrow* it and be who I really was. But that day never came until, finally, I decided to stop waiting for it.

I'd gone back to using that off-campus bar again, and I was now using it too often and I knew it. The sexual pleasure of my adventures there was getting too intense and I began to fear where they might take me. In a desperate attempt to rescue myself, the next time my urge to go there surfaced, I stopped at a pay phone en route and called up the police, anonymously, and reported the place. "You should close it down!" I said.

"Sorry," replied the officer on the other end. "We've got other priorities."

What-the-hell: if they don't care, why should I? And I went back there and continued using it.

A few months later, I stopped by right after noon and I was surprised by how few men were present.

Strange, I thought. But, then, it was the middle of the day and it usually didn't get active until later on, so I paid it no attention and began to cast about in the shadows for a partner.

A slightly older man approached me, well over college age, and he had a cruel look to his face which I found repellant, so I walked away.

He followed me and I retreated again. When he approached me the third time, I turned to him and demanded, "Why don't you butt-out?"

A look of shock crossed his face. "Butt-out? Butt-out?"

His hand suddenly went into his back pocket and he pulled out a badge. "POLICE! You're under arrest!"

My whole world dropped away. Grabbing me by my arm, he hustled me though a side exit into the blinding light of day where a partner in plain clothes came over from a nearby police car and helped handcuff me and place me in the back seat. I was driven down to the nearby station and booked on a charge so ugly that it smelled: *Lewd conduct in a public place.*

Out on bail, I later returned to court and after a humiliating ordeal there paid a fine.

I should have known that this was my wakeup call and that I had to get help. But to do so would have required that I fully face what I had become and I was too afraid of what I might see to do that. But I never went back to that bar again, and even stopped looking for hitchhikers all the time.

Good Word, Bad Word

The lessons you can draw from this story are pretty clear. There are certain conversations that children should never have with strangers. Conversations about their sexual habits and interests are two of them: they're no one else's business and the child who finds themselves in the company of a stranger who asks about those things should get away from that kind of stranger immediately: leave the Chat Room, get off the Internet, get out of his car at the very next corner. The only proper reply to a question from a stranger about a child's sexual interests is "*Goodbye.*"

Hitchhiking is dangerous. It could cost your child their life. It should never be done. Hitchhiking at night is even more dangerous, or near secluded areas. A child should never seek or accept a ride from a stranger.

Does this mean that you should never trust your child with the man or woman who wants to be around him? The Youth Group Counselor, the Athletic Coach, the Minister or Clergyman?

No. But it means there are signs you have a right to look for that may tell you that your child will be *safe*.

One of them is the man who also always has a woman present, and vice versa; always has other kids—*and adults*—around at the same time, and doesn't take a child anywhere alone.

Those may not make dangerous adults safe, but at least it keeps them from striking and if they want to strike and are deprived long-enough, they'll leave your child alone and go elsewhere. Lucifer is *not* a lo-cal guy.

Make a sacred promise to your child: that if they ever find themselves being approached or touched by an older person in any way that makes them feel uncomfortable and they tell you, under no circumstances will you react in anger or distress, because those are the reasons why your child will never tell you. No matter how hard it may be to do so, *force* yourself to at least seem calm for sixty seconds. Use them to tell your child instead that it was not their fault that whatever happened, happened, and that they did the right thing in telling you because you will see to it that it never happens again.

And then contact the appropriate agencies for assistance.

*   *   *

Questions for Group Discussion

1. Why don't some children say 'no' to the sexual predator who solicits them? What could parents do to make sure that their children do?

2. What kind of children does the child molester typically seek? And what could a parent or care-provider do to prevent their child from becoming that type?

3. If laws aren't enough to stop the compulsive sex offender, would you favor leniency if he turned himself in? If so, under what terms?

4. Should mental health counselors be required to report a client who admits to having molested a child, even if that will keep potential clients from coming in for help?

5. Should members of the clergy be required to report those who admit to molesting a child in confession?

Chapter Three

Victims and Consequences

In the months following my arrest, my wife and I parted and then divorced. I bought a camper van, wandered for a while across the United States and back again, returning to the West Coast where I wandered for the better part of the next ten years. I encountered shamanism, the Human Potential Movement, Free Sex and Zen Buddhism. Strange as it may seem, I also participated in a bisexual orgy scene for a while with girls of college age.

I was never just a *child molester*, I liked to get lost in sex and took it whenever I could, like the alcoholic who will drink anything that will get him intoxicated. And after I had encountered all of these experiences, I married again in my forties and went down to Los Angeles to go to law school: a mid-life career change. That's where I met Snap and found out what happened to boys like those I had molested.

It was at a part-time job that I took, over at a counseling center in Hollywood, where I came to clerk for a number of its attorneys who defended clients when they got into trouble. Snap used to hang out in the lobby there, as a lot of the gay kids did, and that's where I first encountered him.

In his late teens or early twenties, he had been on *The Street*, as we called it, since Age 14: nearby Santa Monica Boulevard, where in between gay bars and gay bathhouses, and a beat that never stopped, teenage male hustlers regularly plied their trade. With chestnut-colored hair and a lean build, he had the wild animal look of someone who had been on the hunt for a long time. I saw him sitting outside my office one day, when I got ready to go on a coffee break at the fast foods restaurant next door. I'd seen him a couple of times before and now he was giving me the 'hi' sign, so I motioned for him to come along. It was at the restaurant that he told me his story.

The One-Hundred Dollar Trick

"I ran away from home when I was just a kid," he said, in between quick gulps of coffee. He'd come from somewhere in the Midwest.

"I got on the highway and stuck out my thumb and the first dude who picked me up was a businessman of some sort, an older guy, like, in his fifties. He offered me ten bucks for sex."

Ten dollars was a lot of money in those days, especially to a runaway kid. "Afterwards," Snap said, taking another quick gulp, "he let me off and drove away and I felt that crisp new ten dollar bill in my pocket and thought, 'I got myself a *career* now!'"

Other older men quickly obliged his need for customers and by the time he'd crossed the country he was in the company of a man who lived in L.A. "In Hollywood," Snap said, with excitement. "This dude had a pad high up in the hills, with a swimming pool and a stereo and a color TV that I could watch all I wanted. He was gone all day, so I just smoked dope and got high and it was good."

What about sex?

"Oh, yeah. We had that too. At first, he wanted it every night, but I told him, 'Hey, man: I'm just a kid! Take it easy.'" Snap laughed slyly. "He backed off after that."

He took another gulp of coffee.

Since the man had financially supported Snap and now Snap was on The Street, it was pretty obvious their relationship had ended and I was curious to know why he thought it had. Snap lit up a cigarette and took a quick drag. "Aw," he said, exhaling. "He tried to 'father' me—wanted me to go to school, 'make something of myself.' It was the same old crap I'd heard at home, so we finally broke up."

But I'd already heard otherwise from Snap's counselor: the boy's adult companion had gotten his feelings hurt when Snap had told him that he could never be anyone's 'father' as all he wanted to do was have sex with boys, and the man had insisted that he leave.

Snap admitted it when I repeated this. "Yeah," he said, wearing a grin of embarrassment. "But it worked out okay. He called a friend of his and arranged for me to stay there, and this other dude came over and picked me up and I went home with him."

It soon became the same story all over again: sex at first, then a fumbling try by a child molester to become a surrogate father. Quarrels and then an ouster. Snap went to a third man's home and, this time, the man wanted Snap to be a party favor for three of his friends one night and Snap got so scared that he ran away.

He made it down to Hollywood Boulevard, where he tried to panhandle passers-by for enough to eat, but got nothing. Then a tall, thin Black kid, just a few years older than Snap, wearing a golden earring and a long fake gold necklace came up to him. He'd been watching him and thought that Snap was trying to sell himself.

"Chi-al? You ain' never gonna score here. This ain't the place for that kind of action."

When Snap tried to explain, his listener didn't care and quickly tutored him. "Go down to Santa Monica Boulevard. That's where all the trade is, and you trick there. You'll make out fine."

Snap was hungry and did as he was told, and that first night he got a man to rent him a motel room that he could stay in after they were done, and enough money for a decent meal at a nearby restaurant.

The following night, Snap went out on The Street again and scored once more. Soon, he met other boys like himself who schooled him further. When they heard his story of what had happened with the first men he had lived with, their reactions were automatic. "You should have robbed him!"

Many such boys did, and the files of the West Hollywood Sheriff's Office bulge with complaints from nearby hillside residents who report that they have had their car and jewelry taken by their former *houseboy*.

Snap was invited to pool his money with the other boy-prostitutes and their life became one of fast foods, fast sex, powerful drugs, shared motel rooms and soon sex with each other whenever they could afford to get high together.

They had dreams. All hustlers on The Street in Hollywood have dreams, always centered about their regular customers—the ones who always come back, at least at first.

"He's gonna take me to Hawaii!"

"He's gonna get me in The Movies!"

"He's gonna buy me a car!"

"He once gave me a Hundred Dollars!"

"Bull shit! No one ever gave you a hundred dollars. You're just a five-dollar-fuck!"

"Fuck you!"

"Fuck *you*!"

Snap became a pro and that's how he did it.

We finished our coffee and I went back to my office. A month later he called me from the county jail.

"I'm in *trouble*, man. Big trouble. I'm scared shitless. You gotta come down here and help me. Please! I think they're going to gang-rape me!"

I got in my car and went down immediately and he told me what had happened.

Among the regular customers on The Street there was a retired businessman from The Valley who came into Hollywood every weekend and rented a room in a Sunset Strip motel where he brought the boys he'd bought for sex. He'd already had Snap several times and no longer wanted him, but when he saw Snap coming out of another room, he hailed him over and said, "Look: you go upstairs, to the third floor. There's a dude up there who will pay you *one-hundred bucks* to have sex with him."

He flashed Snap a fifty-dollar bill and explained. "He paid me this much just to get him a kid. Go do him and the hundred's yours."

Snap was already pretty spaced-out from just having had sex, and he was also high on drugs. His judgment was flawed. All he could think of was finally being able to say that he'd had a one-hundred dollar trick—for that was magic on The Street; it meant that you were *extra*-special—so he agreed to do what his contact suggested and went upstairs.

When the door opened, he found himself being greeted by a man with dark eyebrows and a menacing look who motioned him in with a flick of his head. The moment the door closed behind Snap, the man bolted it shut. That's when Snap saw two other men emerging from the kitchen on the other side of the room.

And one of them held a whip.

Snap grabbed a nearby table lamp and hurled it at the men, kicked the one in the groin who'd let him in, pulled the bolt and tore the door back open and fled downstairs, furious with the retired businessman for having set him up.

He pounded on the door to the man's room and when it opened he hurled his fist at the man's face. The man ducked and then quickly shoved his way past Snap to run away. Snap chased after him.

The man got into the motel's elevator and its doors closed just before Snap caught up with him.

Snap raced upstairs and when the elevator doors opened, he leaped inside and began to beat the man as the man frantically pressed the Down button. The two of them descended together as Snap pummeled the man's face.

Snap was wearing a leather bracelet that night, with stainless steel spikes on it, and they left the man blind.

The beaten man slumped to the floor, unconscious from the pain, and Snap dug into the man's pockets and grabbed his car keys. When the elevator reached the ground floor, Snap jumped out, raced over to the man's car, and drove it away. For the rest of that night, he drove in huge meaningless circles all over Hollywood, not certain where he was going or what he should do. At dawn, he returned the car to the motel where police were waiting. Now, he was in the adult section of Los Angeles County Jail and he was afraid that he was going to be gang-raped.

"Please!" he begged me, speaking into a telephone from his side of the thick glass window in the Visitors Room. "Get me out of here!"

He looked quickly to his left and right and then leaned forward as he said into the telephone, *"I'm not really an adult. I'm only seventeen!"*

The moment I told the deputies that, three of them took him away. He was driven right over to a juvenile facility and placed there until his court appearance.

We all thought. But five days later, I received a call from a lady who worked at the juvenile detention facility, an older woman who had labored in Juvenile Hall for years and knew all about kids.

"He ain't no *ju*-venile," she said. "His face-hair growin' back too fast foh ah *ju*-venile. You bettah come on down here."

I did, and Snap confessed that he was really nineteen.

I called his Public Defender and was told to meet him in court that afternoon, where a judge appointed me to assist the court by getting in contact with Snap's family to verify his correct age. They let me talk to Snap and he gave me an address for some relatives who lived way out at the northernmost end of Los Angeles, in the San Fernando Valley. I drove out there that night, only to find that the street he gave me ended in the surrounding desert before it had a number even remotely like the one he had supplied. Snap had conned the system.

And the court wasn't having any more of it. He wound up being tried as an adult and was given six years and sent to San Quentin.

If he survived it.

The Lessons & What You Can Do About It

Snap's fate was what made me question whether teenagers should have the *right* to have sexual relations with whomever they wished, as I'd come to believe by this point, like all child molesters. Although I have met several successful, well-adjusted Gay men who have told me that they had love affairs with adults when they were minors, and still value the experience, more often what I learn is that it's only a damaging event to the young person involved. Afterwards, the boys or girls who get into these kinds of relationships have been left *sexualized*: with an appetite for something they aren't able to handle with balance yet and, only too often, another adult predator comes along to exploit them. Soon, they can no longer respect adults as authority figures, leaving them unable to be controlled by teachers or counselors.

Left in confusion as to their own sexual identities, they frequently drop out of school, which leaves them unable to function adequately in society, so they turn to crime. Often, as it did with Snap, they become teen prostitutes, or worse, and may even wind up being sent to prison like him.

But I was still so unconscious of all this that I didn't realize I had just met my first victim who was showing me the damage that people like me caused to people like him.

You can put a stop to child prostitution. *Children of the Night* is a private, non-profit, tax-exempt organization founded in 1979 to rescue children from street prostitution. With a nationwide, toll-free 24-hour hotline, a group home, placement in foster homes, drug programs, mental health programs, special education programs and jobs with independent living—all supported by private donations—the organization claims an 80% success rate in getting kids out of prostitution and keeping them free from going back to it. Working with what it calls "a small but committed group of detectives, FBI agents and prosecutors" across the country on the "child prostitution circuit," Children of the Night prosecutes the pimps who exploit such children while helping to locate missing children and get them returned to their families.

For further information, go to their website at *http://childrenofthenight.org* Or phone the organization at its national hotline: 1-800-551-1300.

If you live outside the United States, phone the police and ask them who is doing the same kind of work there and help them. The danger, otherwise, could reach you: if you don't stop child prostitution, some of its members may approach a child in your family and entice them "to make a few quick dollars." For child prostitutes can also become accomplices to child sex predators that way, and you don't have to permit that.

Something Coming Down the Street: Incest

Law school began late that summer. It was to be an intensive, two-year program, requiring full-time attention by all of its students, but I wouldn't let my connection with the counseling center go. It was too exciting—the pulse of the place, its nonstop phone calls, lawyers from all over the country asking us for advice—and so was the lifestyle that I found with it. *The sex! The drugs! The Boys!*

The Street.

Lectures began late that summer and homework assignments were given out daily: reading and analyzing key cases in various fields of law. On my first exams I couldn't seem to give my professors what they wanted and my initial grades were not good ones.

That fall I transferred out of the intensive program and into the more traditional four-year-long one, given at night. Perhaps if I went slower I'd do better. But my home life made that impossible. My new wife and I fell into a love-hate relationship almost from the beginning and, like many mutually-injuring couples, all we were doing now was keeping score. We tried to break up, but an early pregnancy brought us back together for another try.

It didn't work and as my law work—both at the Center with its attorneys, and in law school—consumed more of my time, my new wife seemed to become more and more alienated from me. We started to take Lamaze birth training together, but our continuous quarreling kept us from completing it.

A month after my daughter was born, my wife took the child with her and left me for the Christmas holidays. When she returned, our marriage began its terminal phase, like a car that keeps moving when you turn off its motor, simply by momentum. A couple of years later it finally came to a stop when my wife left me for another man and filed for divorce.

Even then, I remained willing to do anything to win her back if only because our relationship had allowed me to maintain a lifelong fiction of mine that I was really as normal as anyone else. The result was that, when our divorce proceeded and she offered me a shared custody arrangement under which our daughter would live part of each week with her and part of each week with me—creating regular times when my wife and I would see each other as the child was exchanged between us—*times when I might win her back!*—I eagerly grasped at it.

Such hopes turned out to be an illusion however, as my wife had no interest in coming back this time and I simply wouldn't allow myself to accept that fact. Over the next couple of years, she grew even more distant and the amount of time that the child was staying with me increased each week until, by the end, the child was living with me all week long and with her mother only on weekends.

I soon came to feel "trapped" into taking care of the child—'more like a grandfather,' I told myself, wallowing in self-pity. I lost all sense of self-esteem. I no longer considered myself attractive to anyone. I felt rejected as, over and over again, my ex-wife came to drop the child off or pick her back up again and remained deaf to my pleas to stay. Working as one of the cocktail waitresses at a glamorous nightspot on the Sunset Strip, every time she came by she was dressed like a million dollars. And every time she turned me down and left, it was like being rejected all over again.

I began to drink more than before. I began using recreational drugs more than before. Isolated and without friends, I soon became desperately lonely.

My daughter increasingly filled that loneliness until I found her to be more a source of love than my ex-wife. Like countless men before me, and countless men to come, that is when I began to look to my daughter for the kind of emotional relationship I could no longer have with her mother.

It wasn't long before I crossed the forbidden line. The same destructive urges as before—that had taken everything else from my life—returned again and, once again, took what I loved the most.

        *   *   *

In September of 1985 I had only recently received my law degree and moved into a brand-new apartment in West Hollywood. I was working on a mayhem trial in the superior court. The defendant had injured her husband during a family altercation and the woman who was the deputy district attorney on the case and I had gotten to respect each other's work as the hearing progressed.

When I got the court's permission to go out to the women's prison to see if it had any of the counseling programs I insisted the defendant needed, my opponent asked to come along and I welcomed her doing so. We drove out together, spending the day there. Upon our return to Los Angeles, I dropped her off at her downtown office and returned to my new residence, only to learn from messages left on my answering machine that my father had passed away that very day.

Shaken, I called the D.A. up and told her. She was immediately sympathetic and that helped stabilize me. I phoned my ex-wife and asked her to take our child for the weekend, as I would be involved in helping my mother attend the funeral. We agreed to meet afterwards, at my mother's house, when the child would be returned.

My ex-wife arrived that day as promised, but immediately implored me to speak with her in private for a moment, while our child waited in another room. She was shaken and I could see it. Once behind closed doors, she told me that our daughter had accused me of having molested her.

Although she would later insist—while acting as a witness for the prosecution—that I didn't confirm it until after she'd argued with me, I recall admitting it immediately. "Thank God it's out," I said. For now I could expel it and seek professional help as all my fears of getting caught had just been realized.

It's easy to fault such a person for not having sought professional help earlier, even if imprisonment is what they risk by doing so these days. But that is asking for a degree of courage from someone who is already so lost as to make it almost impossible for them to find it. The result is that the children continue to suffer as their victims. Under a law that only seeks social vengeance, it is the child victims who are punished.

My ex-wife quickly told me she'd already seen an attorney and had the child's allegations reported to police. "They're looking for you now," she announced.

"Better call in our daughter," I said. For, after having worked on cases just like this, I knew that I might never see her again and I didn't want her left with any unnecessary guilt if that happened.

When she was escorted into the room I told her that she had done the *right* thing in telling, and that she should never forget it. "I'll always love you," I assured her. We hugged, I said it again, and then the two of them went home and I returned to my apartment. The next day, I called my deputy district attorney friend and asked her to meet me after work. "It's personal," I said. "And you're going to hear about it through the system, so I'd rather you heard it from me first."

We met at a small restaurant nearby and I told her what had happened with my ex-wife the night before. I couldn't complete the telling before I broke down in tears, and so did she. A moment later, when I tried to go on, she stopped me. "Don't say anymore," she cautioned me, clutching a handkerchief now. "I'm still a prosecutor. Have you got a lawyer?"

"No," I replied. "Can you recommend one?"

A former colleague, now in private practice, was suggested and the next day I called and asked that attorney to arrange for my surrender.

Several days later, my lawyer and I went to police headquarters and I was booked and then released on bail. My ex-wife and daughter were also there, and I told my ex-wife to contact the court and choose a therapist for our child from its list of approved specialists. "I will pay for it," I said and when I went to court I entered a plea of guilty. In return, the court delayed my sentencing hearing for almost a year so that the child's doctor could have all the time he needed to take care of her, while I got a therapist of my own to work with me.

It's a good thing that I had disclosed my misconduct to that deputy D.A. or I might later have been tempted to beat the case, for when the police interviewed my daughter she told them that a babysitter had *also* molested her, and it would have been easy to have some attorney put her on the stand and get her so confused as to which of us did what that I probably would have walked free. She was only five years old.

But what would that have done to her? What could I have gained, had I tried to save myself by falsely calling her a liar?

I've never regretted my decision to tell the truth and I urge anybody in a similar situation to do the same thing. It's called an Act of Decency and it may be your first, so try it on and see if it doesn't feel better than the kind you've been doing.

In any case of sexual abuse within the family—even by a person who comes to act as a surrogate member of the family—the heart of the crime is that it isn't at all like abuse caused by a stranger. Rather, the perpetrator here has taken on some very cherished role in the child's life and, almost always, it's one they tried to perform.

Not that it's meant to excuse the situation, but only to understand it, one has to remember that, in addition to molesting the child, an in-family perpetrator probably also fed the child, housed the child, got medicine for the child when ill, maybe took the child to doctors and dentists and even attended school plays.

They developed an *emotional bond* with the child, whether misused or not. Like mine, with my daughter, it may not have been a healthy one. They may, like me, have believed that they loved the child. But to say—as some prosecutors have—that the perpetrator in a family situation "only" meant to take advantage of the child—is to damage the child even more, by calling the child's feelings about this person untrue when there is rarely, if ever, any evidence whatsoever to suggest the perpetrator was only seeking a relationship in which he could molest the child. Rather, the relationship starts as a good one and only gradually decays as the perpetrator loses control of himself. Depravity is a journey, not a jump.

Like it or not—and this is tough stuff—the child in a family sexual abuse situation has just had their first sexual relationship in life and to only cheapen that, *as improper as it was for the adult to have sought it*, is to tell the child that they aren't loveable, and that should be a crime, too.

The defendant's misdeeds are evidence-enough to convict. It isn't necessary to crucify the child too and no parent should permit that to be done. The child has just lost a friend because that friendship was defective. They shouldn't lose the other parent's support. Rather, the child should be comforted in their sorrow for a love that's been lost, *even if should have been,* for their sorrow is real and they need their other parent as their friend while they grieve for that loss.

When the child's grief is past, they can be helped in understanding that they deserved a better love than they got this time, and assured that they will get one in the future because they deserve it. Until then, they shouldn't be allowed to stop believing in themselves because they've just lost someone else. For if they lose faith in themselves, they will lose faith in their life and never have the really fine life that they deserve.

That's the support I hoped her therapist was giving her, while I also did what I could for myself. Hoping to avoid a sentence of imprisonment, I did what almost all such people do in cases like this, and enrolled myself in a sex offender therapy group so that its doctor might testify in favor of my being left in his care under the supervision of a probation officer in the community as my only penalty. Each week I attended meetings with others just like me at his office, which were enormously painful as, previously, I had been the one to send men to groups like that in my alternative sentencing practice.

I also worked with the child's doctor, telling him anything he wanted to know so that he could help my daughter deal with everything that was going on in her life now. This, too, was enormously painful for me as I was so ashamed of what I'd let myself become.

It was painful for my child too, as now she missed me.

Because of this, the doctor felt that I should continue to see her, but only with a court-approved monitor present—and I did so whenever visits were scheduled. But no matter how hard the monitor tried to stay in the background on those occasions, their being there at all couldn't help but make them very awkward ones.

I'm sure it was very difficult for them, too.

As the months went by, visits began to be scheduled by the doctor less and less frequently as he let the bonds lessen between my daughter and me, while building new ones between her and her mother.

My sentencing practice vanished within a week of my arrest, and in the sudden vacuum of each day I began to feel a sense of dread, as if 'something' I couldn't exactly picture was coming down my street for me, rolling my whole life up before it as it did so. But I couldn't figure out what it was.

A lawyer I knew warned me that I was *not* going to get probation. "They're going to *crucify* you!" he said. "You worked for the courts. You know the rule: if you're part of The System and mess-up, they make an example of you. They're going to send you to prison, and you may not survive it."

In my fear that he might be right, I began thinking of suicide. A short time later, under the strain, my appendix burst and I was hospitalized.

After I recovered from surgery and got back to my apartment, I began taking long walks around my neighborhood and started to mourn the fact that, up until then, I hadn't taken the time to appreciate any of life's most ordinary things, like a new blade of grass springing up or a bird hopping across a lawn. Would it be too late now, I asked myself, to begin living that kind of life?

A Flash at Dawn

I came upon a non-sectarian meditation group in a house nearby, led by an anonymous man with an anonymous past. He had the bright blonde hair of a Scandinavian and always wore a white shirt and white slacks. In his early thirties and with a slim build, he had an accent I couldn't place. Some said he came from one country, others said he came from another. Speaking to a congregation of recovering addicts and others one could only call the walking wounded, he said that even when your life is smashed you still have a choice: "to be but a broken piece of a master, or a master-piece."

I began attending his meditation group weekly and then an auxiliary one that his followers held without him on a second night. When it was announced that there would be a weekend-long session, with a private audience with him for all who attended, I eagerly signed up believing that, perhaps, he had the ability to summon some sort of *supernatural* intervention that might save me from being imprisoned.

They took me in to see him on the last afternoon of that weekend. He was in a small room, seated on a high-backed rattan chair. In front of him on the floor, there was a cushion for me to use. I sat down upon it and looked up at him. He stared down at me and in a loud whisper asked, "*What do you want?*"

All of my plans to seek his help through asking for some sort of *miracle* suddenly vanished and in their place a spontaneous declaration burst forth from my lips.

"*To return to the Heart of God and never leave it again!*"

It was a plea for refuge and, a month later, when I was finally in front of my judge to be sentenced, it was granted: *but not the way I expected.*

The hearing itself took several weeks before it could be concluded, for the courts at that time were so overcrowded with cases to be heard that they had to hear them all, piecemeal. Some had time deadlines—by which they had to be heard or thrown out—and others, like mine, did not. The result was that they got most of the court's time each day and my type only got a half-hour or an hour, early in the morning.

A further result was that, instead of being concluded after having had no more than four or five full days of hearing at the most, it was stretched out over almost that many weeks. At one point I seriously began to wonder if I would ever be sentenced, or just spend years in legal limbo, coming before the court for a sentencing that might never take place.

That was an illusion, of course. But when my case had been fully presented, it kept me from realizing that my sentence was just about to be decided, while I thought there might still be another week or so to go. As a result, when I left the courtroom on that final Friday, I merely looked forward to the weekend and gave no thought about what might happen when I returned to court the following Monday.

I should have for, on Saturday, my attorney phoned me at home.

"I don't mean to sound too pessimistic, but if I were you I'd use this weekend to pack up your things—you know, just in case things don't go our way on Monday."

"Sure," I replied. But I wasn't really worried. One of the advantages of being in a state of denial is that you don't worry about *anything* you should worry about. That is also, of course, its major disadvantage. But I thought it wouldn't do any harm to go through my apartment and tidy it up a bit, throwing out stuff I no longer needed, and putting a few things in boxes.

That evening, I went out as usual and had a very nice dinner with a young man I met at a restaurant known to have young men like him available to men like me. We went home afterwards, had sex, slept together overnight and had a nice brunch the following Sunday morning before we parted, agreeing to get back in touch in a few days. As far as I could see, there was really nothing to worry about.

I was in *complete* denial. But something deeper than the personal 'I' within all of us knew better and, that Sunday night—or, more accurately, at dawn on Monday morning, only hours before I would be returning to court—it announced its intention to seize the throne I had occupied so irresponsibly, by sending me a dream:

It was dark out on the desert and the sands softly rippled away in front of me. Up ahead, I could just barely make out the figure of a woman shrouded in a dark robe from head to foot, seated on top of a boulder. In her arms she cradled a young man who was unconscious and wearing only a white loincloth. All about us the silence was total. Suddenly, from beyond the horizon far in back of her, there was a silent burst of white light—like the kind I'd seen as a kid on my newspaper route early in the morning, when they were still testing atomic bombs in Nevada, 500 miles away. It quickly expanded, like a flower opening itself to the day, then folded back up again and the darkness returned. Immediately afterwards, and directly overhead, I heard a man's deep voice call out of the darkness with one booming word:

"HOLOCAUST!"

I bolted awake in my bed. It was just before dawn and I was alone.

What kind of a dream was that?

I threw back the satin sheets, stepped into my slippers and grabbed my maroon bathrobe hanging on the bedpost. Quickly plunging both my arms into it and lashing it around myself, I walked into the adjoining bathroom. Hot water full of bubbles immediately soaked the thick cotton washcloth and I pressed it against my face to melt away the crust of sleep.

I brushed my teeth, then made my way toward the kitchen to brew a cup of coffee.

Cigarette!

I walked into the living room that had also served as my law office. A dark mahogany desk and leather-upholstered chair sat there and I grabbed the pack I'd left next to my wooden in-box the night before. A flick of a nearby lighter and I was sucking in all the assurance I needed.

The Dream: *Holocaust!*

While I hardly thought of myself as a practicing Jew in those days, the word *holocaust* was a buzz word, one that always caused shadows to quickly flicker past in my mind—of dim memories from earliest childhood, when relatives spoke among themselves in hushed tones in another room, after making certain I wasn't about—of other relatives, still in Europe, who had disappeared...*in all the ashes.*

What could it mean? Why should I have such a dream, especially today, when I had to go back into court to see what the judge was going to do with me?

My eyes wandered over to a nearby bookcase and that's when I saw a celebrated fortune-telling book from ancient China that I'd bought years before: *The I Ching (Book of Changes).*

I'd tried to use it when I first got it, but it had never worked for me.

But, *perhaps,* I thought, this morning it might work and tell me what that dream meant, and whether it had anything to do with what's going to happen in court today.

Hurriedly, I got up and brought the book over to my desk, and went through the brief ritual it required: of casting three coins six times to seek its answer, writing down how many heads and tails I got each time. When they were totaled, a chart inside the book led me to the page that would give me my answer and I quickly turned to it.

A prison is foreseen, it said. *You will be gone a long time.*

"Bull-shit!" I said to myself, slamming the book shut. "I'm not going to believe that!"

I got up from my desk and went to shave, shower and dress before leaving for court. I was a *modern* man and I wasn't about to believe in such foolish superstitions!

The courtroom was almost empty when I arrived. Several court-watchers sat in back and I took a seat at the defense table, up in front. All of my character witnesses—neighbors, a couple of colleagues from my work, members of my family—had already appeared on my behalf and now were gone. When my attorney came in, I felt terribly alone.

The judge entered and we all stood up. He was a large, beefy man with a ruddy complexion and there was a very stern expression on his face today. Things didn't look good: only the prosecutor was smiling.

The judge tapped his gavel lightly and said, with mock weariness: "I suppose we'll have the standard plea for mercy now."

My attorney stood up and answered, "Yes, your honor."

"Proceed."

But, halfway through my lawyer's presentation, the judge halted it. "I've heard enough. He's going to prison. Today!"

I had been sentenced both above and below and was given ten years and taken away as a sex offender. The only question left was whether I would come back as one.

The Lessons

While every incest case is different in some ways, there are certain characteristics that many of them have in common: a dysfunctional marriage, a future offender who is sexually insecure, and a child who comes to be used as an emotional surrogate by one of the partners for the other. If you see such a marriage in your family, urge its members to immediately get professional counseling and restore it to health, or completely end it so the child doesn't become its next casualty.

If you want parents already trapped in incest to be able to get professional help, so the child can be saved from further molestation as soon as possible, tell your legislators that you want the law changed so that no parent who comes to an appropriate clinician or counselor for help after the *first* time they lose control is ever given a prison sentence.

If you want to make certain that the child molester sent to prison doesn't come back as one, read the next few chapters about prisons and what a convicted offender is likely to find there that should be supported in some cases, and re-examined in others. If you really want to be certain that your neighborhood will be left free from repeat sex offenders, the place to begin is in the programs that prisons now offer in some places and should offer in all, because the prisoner held today may be living near you tomorrow.

*   *   *

Questions for Group Discussion

1. What should the neighborhood do when it sees a young boy suddenly living with an adult male?
2. What responsibility, if any, should motels and hotels have when an adult male suddenly returns to his room with an underage child?
3. What kind of man is likely to engage in incest? What kind of signals do you think you could spot?
4. Should the incest offender be exempt from being sent to prison, so as to repair and preserve the family? If so, what safeguards should be in place?
5. What help could you give to the incest victim, if one were known to you in your neighborhood (or family)? What help could you give to the child's mother? To the offending parent?

Chapter Four

The Man With Nothing Left to Lose

I'd been given a chance to escape. Just after the judge had said he was going to send me to prison—but not yet for how long—he received a signal from his courtroom reporter. Her shorthand typing machine was running out of tape and the Judge called a five-minute recess for her to refill it. I walked outside of the courtroom and stood in the hallway. Almost directly across from me, the door to the building's stairwell was wide open, with its bright "EXIT" sign tempting me.

I'd worked in that building for several years now and knew that all I'd have to do is walk across—go through that doorway—and take the steps down to the first floor, walk briskly through the lobby and get across the street to where my car was parked. And then I could go…

…where?

My mind flashed back to those times during law school when a criminal attorney called to tell me he had a client who was now a fugitive and wanted to turn himself in. Usually, it was a man who had been on probation or parole, or on bail awaiting trial, who had bolted rather than face it. All I had to do was meet the man somewhere and drive him down to the criminal courthouse, where I'd walk him in to the appropriate court after first having telephoned its bailiff to let him know we were coming.

It was a simple procedure. Once in court, a deputy public defender would be summoned to stand with the man before the judge, who then set a date for a formal hearing *and then released the man until that time.*

Why not? Obviously, he wasn't going to run, for he had just turned himself in!

But on those drives down to the courthouse with such men, I'd heard their stories of what living like a fugitive had been like.

You can never stay in one place too long. You use a different name wherever you go. You can't use your Social Security number, so you work under-the-table at whatever they'll pay you. You don't trust anybody. You're always looking over your shoulder to see if anyone's following you. When you go to sleep at night, you can't help wondering if the cops will come busting through your doorway before you wake back up. So, you can't settle down. You can't fall in love with anyone. You can't build any kind of a life. All you can do is stay lonely.

It's the loneliness that finally causes so many of them to turn themselves back in. That's why I knew that, if I tried to escape, all I'd do is become lost in that loneliness and so I stepped back from it, leaving me only one place to go and that was state prison.

It's a good thing I made that choice for, just at that moment, I felt someone's eyes on me, up the hallway, and I turned to look. It was the Prosecutor. He was watching me. *He'd been watching me the whole time!*

The Rite of Expulsion

The bailiff came out and told everyone that court was ready to resume. I walked back in and was sentenced—just before I felt the soft grip behind me of a man's hand on one of my wrists. And then the quick cold embrace of a handcuff.

All the insignia of social membership were about to be stripped away from me. My belt was taken off, my shoelaces removed, my pockets emptied. When my car keys were spilled onto the table in front of me, my attorney said, "I'll call your family and have them come get your car."

My lease would soon be terminated for non-payment of rent, my furniture and personal effects removed from the premises, my utility bills left to lapse, my credit cards cancelled, mail would pile up in my mail box until it was full—by which time the postal delivery person would have heard from the apartment house manager that "*He was put in prison! His family told me when they came over to remove his goods!*" My telephone line would be disconnected, my checking account closed for *lack of activity*. My safe deposit box would be opened by the bank when it next became unpaid and my valuables kept somewhere and, when not claimed, vanish.

Within just a few months no entry would be left in any record in the city to suggest that I existed. Even the courthouse would ship its records out. I was banished from the everyday world and it would no longer know of me. I would be taken, instead, to another world, whose entrance is concealed carefully by a paneled door in the court, up front, in the side of a wall, which opens to admit the newly-convicted to a flight of stairs he takes down to find that he is now in another building held *inside* of this one.

This inner building is the jail in the criminal courthouse to which all convicted persons are funneled from similar doorways in each of the court-rooms on several floors, and it has its own hallways, lavatories, control booths with deputy sheriffs in them, and of course jail cells. It's an entire world of its own *under* the courts. An under-world.

At the bottom of the stairs, there was a glass-enclosed booth with some officers inside. One of them spoke to me through a loudspeaker.

"Turn to your right, keep walking until you come to a door, and then halt until the door is opened. Then go inside and keep to yourself!"

I did as he directed and walked thirty steps until I came to a door that was electronically unlatched and then opened. When I stared inside, I saw forty or fifty men, all dressed in county jail blue jumpsuits, sitting on rows of flat wooden benches or standing around, looking back at me as I was the only one in civilian clothes—which told them I'd just been sentenced. To one side, there was a Deputy Sheriff.

"Enter!"

I walked in and he stopped me and removed my handcuffs, then directed me to go take a seat.

I felt too low to even sit on a bench, so I chose the floor next to the end of one, in a corner. *I just wanted to die!*

A young Latino, with a big mound of dark wavy hair, was sitting on the edge of the bench and looked down at me.

"Hey, Man! How much time they give ya?"

I stared back up and glumly replied. "Ten years."

"Man!" he exclaimed. "That ain't nothin'. You're a well-dressed dude, educated. I can see that. When you get to prison, they gonna give you one of those desk-jobs and you'll cut your time to half that."

That was the law in my state then: "Day-for-Day," they called it. For each day that you worked, they removed two days from your sentence instead of just the one you served.

"You ain't gonna do no more than *five* years!"

It might as well have been five centuries.

I took out my pack of cigarettes—they were imported ones—and, instantly, a beehive of men gathered in front of me asking for one. As I didn't know if it would be safe to say 'no,' I let them pass the pack around and it was quickly emptied.

I wouldn't be smoking any more imported cigarettes for a while.

Time walked past like a stranger. When the electronic door opened again, a metal cart with a large cardboard box on top, full of sack lunches, was wheeled in and the sacks were passed around. I was given a cheese sandwich and wearily took a bite.

I looked up at the Latino kid after I'd swallowed it and said, "Tastes like plastic."

He laughed to himself. "They make it that way on purpose so you can shit easier."

I hadn't thought of that.

Late in the day our deputy sheriff told us all to get up. We were taken into the corridor outside until we came to a large freight elevator where other deputies waited to take us further down in small groups to the building's basement where a big black and white Sheriff's bus awaited, with bars on each of its windows. Its front door was opened to receive us.

"Inside!" a deputy barked.

When we were all on board and seated, the bus drove us up a concrete ramp where other deputies opened a large metal gate to let the bus go into the street. In just a few blocks we came to another driveway with another large open gate that closed behind us, and then the bus stopped.

We were at the main county jail where we were quickly unloaded and herded through a nearby doorway into a large room with jail bars at its far end. A half-dozen large, muscular deputies holding billy clubs waited for us. One of the deputies spoke.

"Form a couple of lines!"

We automatically did so and I found a place in the front row. The deputy spoke again.

"Drop 'em!"

All around me the other prisoners began undoing their jail house jump suits and letting them fall to their feet, so I began taking off my clothes. When I got to my underwear, I looked about and saw men shedding their trunks as well and I did the same.

"All right!" said the deputy. "Turn around."

We did so and had our backs facing him. The other deputies came up behind us.

"Bend over!"

We did so.

"Spread 'em!"

The deputies were checking to make sure that no one had brought back any dope or money from the courthouse.

We were sprayed for lice, showered with cold water, given a towel and marched back out to stand in line again, next to our clothes heaped on the floor. We put them back on.

"Alright!" boomed the deputy. "Lissen up! Those jail bars behind me are going to open in a moment and you all know where to go. Anyone new, go with them unless you got a 'problem' of some kind."

That was a cue word I had learned about over at the Counseling Center. The Los Angeles County Jail is one of the most violent places on earth. It holds more prisoners than most penitentiaries, and if you don't want to get hurt you do whatever you have to in order to get protective housing: in special units segregated away from the main population. Telling the deputies that you are Gay is one way to do so and when all the others had left that's exactly what I did. A deputy ordered me to follow him over to a laundry room where my clothes were exchanged for a sky blue jump suit and paper slippers. I quickly changed into them and was then taken outside and put into a small sheriff's van which drove me over to the nearby

Hall of Justice, where the Gay Tank—as it was called—was located, high above the streets of downtown Los Angeles.

The Man with Nothing Left to Lose

The Gay Tank had three floors of cells: Pretty Boy Row, where the good-looking kids were kept so they didn't get raped, Queen's Row, where all of the transvestites were housed, and Stud Row for more aggressive homosexuals. Each row was kept segregated from the others to keep the aggressive men from getting to the boys, and the Queens from getting to either. Since I was neither pretty nor queen, I was sent to Stud Row. That's where I would be kept until there were enough other new arrivals to ship all of us on a sheriff's bus to the state prison intake facility a couple of hours away.

An officer escorted me to a very wide corridor split into two smaller corridors by a wall of jail bars running down its middle. On one side, that made it into a long hallway, through which inmates marched on their way to chow or Sick Call or the Visiting Room. There were a few windows in the wall on that side, where we could look down to the street below and see tiny cars and ant-sized people walking about in the world that had once been ours.

On the other side of the bars, the corridor was filled by a smaller walkway and, next to it, row after row of very compact two-man jail cells. They were old and each was lit by a single bulb on the ceiling—if there was a working fixture there. Within the cell, it was narrow and cramped with one bunk on top of the other, taking up half the space. In the other half, a small washbasin sat next to a metal toilet in the back corner.

My cell was a dark one, my cellmate was in his late twenties, with a pale complexion from being locked up here too long, and he sexually assaulted me that night, then insisted the next morning that he'd never do that again unless I paid him to do so, as if the whole thing had been at my doing. What I wouldn't realize until I'd been through therapy and seen in myself is that he simply didn't understand what had driven him the night before—a blind compulsion and not a reasoned choice. Until the courts understand that's what dominates us, they will continue to sentence us like all others who break the law, when we're not, and we'll keep right on re-offending. Other criminals *choose* to break the law. We don't. We break the law more like a sleepwalker would. Or an addict.

But my cellmate was certainly more awake than I when I asked him what he was in here for. "Don't ask anyone that question," he shot back. First, he said, it was none of my business; second, that it didn't matter.

"We're all in here for the same reason," he went on. "We got caught, and who you were before isn't important. It's who you are now that counts, because that's who we have to live with.

"Besides," he added, "we're all crooks. How could you believe what *any* of us told you?"

There was a daily routine: up before dawn; made to rush down the outside corridor by the deputies so we could go to breakfast, then back to the tier for Sick Call for those who needed it and Visitors for those who had them; lunch, waiting, dinner, nothing, lights out. There were a few old issues of *Reader's Digest* floating around, but not much else. Most of the time was spent just waiting: for jail sentences to end, to be taken to court, or to be taken in chains on busses that would take us to prison.

My first breakfast was cereal, powdered milk, powdered eggs, two pieces of toast with margarine and a spoon full of jelly, some fried potatoes and a cup of very weak coffee. We were made to sit at long rows of tables and eat without speaking—in five minutes—as large deputies walked about, watching us.

Across from me, on the other side of our long table, there was a Pretty Boy and, across from him, down from me by a few seats, an older career criminal. The kid was new; his nervousness betrayed this, and he was trying to eat, but kept looking fearfully over at the older man.

I glanced to my right and saw the man openly leering at him.

The boy could take it no longer and suddenly burst out, "Stop looking at me!"

Instantly, the older criminal grabbed his fork and lunged across the table and slashed the kid's face. A river of blood began erupting from the boy's cheek as the kid belatedly raised his hands to protect himself while the older man was quickly seized from behind by two massive deputies.

"Keep eating!" one of them shouted, as they dragged the older man away. Another deputy gently led the kid out to the dispensary as the boy held bloody paper napkins to his face. He'd have his first jail house scar soon and probably wouldn't be so pretty anymore.

Back on our tier, we were allowed out of our cells to mill around and I saw a very big man seated right in the middle of the concrete floor up ahead, where everyone walked around him very carefully. When I asked my cellmate who that was he told me, "That's a *'Man with Nothing Left to Lose.'* You stay away from him."

"Whadaya mean?" I asked.

He lit a cigarette, took a drag off it and passed it to me. It tasted great.

"It means," he said, "that he's got a sentence so long that he's never coming back. The rumor is that he killed a couple of kids. He's got, like, three life sentences, one after the other. If he ever finishes the first, he does the second; if he finishes that, he does the third. He's in for the whole day. Fuck with him and he'll kill you, 'cause he's got nothing left to lose. What are they going to do? Give him more time? You avoid people like that or you won't survive."

I wondered how many thousands of such men our newer laws were creating now. With all their longer sentences for sex offenders, that threaten so many with lifetimes behind bars who haven't even been caught yet, were child molesters going to be driven into becoming child killers? Why not? The penalty for murder is usually Life and, if you're already facing that, what's to stop you from killing anyone to keep from being caught?

People who rush to support laws increasing prison time even more may not know it, but if they witness a serious-enough crime, *they* may also become the criminal's next victim so that no witnesses are left behind. What are the courts going to do: give the criminal more time when he's already facing *all the time there is*? A sentencing structure based on anger only endangers the public. We need a return to balanced penalties, that seek to punish as appropriate, but not more. We need to have punishments that also give a man a way to redeem himself.

Passover in County Jail

On my second day there my mother came to visit. I was taken to a narrow booth with a stool by a waist-high counter on top of which sat a telephone connecting me to one just like it on her side of the bullet-proof glass window that separated us.

My mother spoke first. "Bob, you're looking well. How are you feeling?"

I didn't want to answer that question truthfully.

She told me that she'd already called officials here, and was going to put forty dollars on my books so I could buy cigarettes and anything else I needed at the jail commissary, but I knew that was just her way of not telling me how very hurt she felt. In the almost twelve months that had elapsed, from the time I gave myself up until now, in spite of numerous times that she and I had gotten together, she had never been able to ask about my offense and I had never been able to bring myself to speak about it to her.

Other men, with similar offenses, would tell me the same thing, coming from families where denial at the dinner table is the norm because the reality of everyone's lives was too frightening to face. Everyone in the family was failing to live out their dreams. None of them were getting the life they really wanted. And everyone was afraid to admit this, so they substituted pretense for fulfillment and came away with inner bank accounts that were always overdrawn.

Conviction of a sex offense isn't just the failure of the individual who commits it. It's also the failure of his entire family and of everyone who had a role in forming him. As Rupert Ross, a Crown Prosecutor serving aboriginal villages in Canada, has reported in his own books, a sex offense is also the failure of the entire tribe and must be addressed that way to be healed. They not only ask that the offender undergo a ritual of penitence, but that everyone else join him in doing so in order that the entire tribe may be restored to its wholeness.

Offenders aren't banished to faraway prisons there. Native peoples say that's too *light* a penalty. They prefer to keep him within the tribe, so he has to face his shame each day while performing community service as well as making restitution to the victim and her family. This doesn't stop until he has earned back his place of honor in the tribe. But, being cultures that dwell in denial, most countries banish people rather than deal directly with the problems they cause and which we still haven't learned how to solve. As a result, those problems only continue to occur as modern societies break down and more offenders are left behind, unhealed. We need to make some changes. The community deserves to have a voice in the sentence imposed in a sex offense case. The opinions of the victim, his or her family, the opinions of the offender's family, other members of the community effected by the case need to be heard. An opportunity for healing has to be a part of the sentence or it is the community that is sentenced to dealing with the offender when he gets back out.

And I needed to change myself. After my visit was over I went back to my tier and grabbed an old copy of some magazine lying on a table by the gate, hoping I'd find something in it that would let me *escape* from facing where I was.

It didn't work. I took it to my cell and, as I lay back on my bunk and tried to read, I couldn't help but be distracted by all the men walking by, outside my cell. I got a nasty look at myself in the mirror of their faces: squalid men who had squandered their lives by chasing nothing but genital urges in their race toward a bottom that has no bottom. Depravity.

Here we all were, ejected from society and sent into this *sewer* to live. I suddenly understood that this was where The Street ended, that this was where it had always been heading.

I felt sickened with self-loathing and quickly made a silent vow to myself that, somehow, I would find the means to make myself into a person who would never have to come back here. That was the moment when I first decided to change.

Later that morning, when my cellmate went to Sick Call and I lay back on the lower bunk with the gate to our cell open, I was just about to doze off when a man appeared there. I blinked my eyes open as he said, "Excuse me."

I sat up in alarm as he continued. "I don't mean to bother you, but I've volunteered to be the Jewish Chaplain's clerk and from your name I assumed you were Jewish."

There was no reason to be fearful.

He continued. "We're going to be celebrating Passover in a few days and I added you to the list of men who will be transported over to the Main Jail for services. I hope you don't mind."

Passover? In County Jail? The Jewish holiday celebrating liberation from slavery? To even think that *my people* would reach out to me at a time like this—when I was in this, this *sewer*—was more than I could accept. Tears of gratitude flooded my eyes.

My visitor understood my sudden need for privacy and quietly left my cell as I covered my face with my hands and wept into them.

Don't think that *God* can't be present in a place filled with men who have committed sexual offenses. The question isn't whether God can accept being with a sex offender. The question is whether a sex offender can accept being with God.

Later that week I was put back into a Sheriff's van and driven over to the Main Jail with several others. There were at least fifty inmates present when I arrived there and I joined them in sitting at long tables in a large room where small prayer books waited at each of our places. Up at the front of the room there was a raised platform on top of which, at a long table of their own, sat the Jewish Chaplain, along with several officials and ladies of the Sisterhood that had donated the sacred foods we were about to eat: matzos, gefilte fish, horseradish, bitter herbs, greens, mixed fruit and nuts, a lamb's shank and roast chicken.

When the Rabbi began the service, I was shocked to see that virtually all of the other men around me—murderers, rapists, thieves, embezzlers—knew how to read the passages written in Hebrew. Only I, with my law school education and master's degree, did not know the language of my own people.

A wish suddenly welled up within me: *If only I could have the time to really learn my religion!*

Some wishes are heard as prayers. And those are granted.

Why Repeat Offenders Keep Repeating

At 4:00 A.M. a couple of weeks later, I was shackled in chains to a long line of other prisoners and loaded onto a sheriff's bus and driven out to the intake facility for the state's prison system. There, one of my state's many penal institutions would be picked for me after counselors had gone over my court file, for there are all kinds of prisons for all kinds of men. Some house factories, inside of which men work. Others have educational programs or major medical services. Some are just human warehouses, and the first task of the prison system is to determine which kind of institution would be most appropriate for each person sentenced into its custody.

Immediately upon entering the building, our chains were removed as guards looked on and directed us to a long counter where one of the clerks turned out to be a former client of mine: a tall mildly-overweight man in his fifties with salt and peppered hair. I'd worked on his sentencing hearing and lost in my bid to keep him out of prison. Now, he was serving time and, as his prison work-assignment, hand-stenciling prisoners' names onto the tabs of what would become their file folders. "See how good my workmanship is?" he asked, hopefully.

He had formerly been the vice president of a statewide bank.

Various other clerks filled out papers on us as we were asked to state our name, date of birth, next of kin—then I was taken in a long line with the other men down a long corridor at the end of which there were three landings of jail cells, each cell housing two men. The cell I was given was on the third landing and already had its other resident: a tall, lanky man in his forties with thinning black hair who hailed from some rural town and was back in prison again. A repeat offender—he said he was a car thief—he was happy to be coming back and talked about the lieutenant he had worked for in prison as if the man had been his father.

He schooled me not to walk next to the edge of our tier when I went to chow with all of the other men.

"Why not?" I asked, naively.

He snorted to himself as we were released for the next meal and clawed our way through everyone to take the stairs down. "So you don't get pushed off by someone who wants to be a 'bad killer' now that he's in here."

I accepted his advice.

After the meal, when we were back in our cell, he lay back on a pillow on the lower bunk and I stood, leaning against the wall across from it and asked him what would happen to me in this place.

"You'll wait," he replied, "like all the rest of us."

"For what?"

"Until you've been seen by a counselor and assigned to a prison." He reached into his shirt pocket and pulled out a small sack of cigarette tobacco, then some papers and sat up to roll himself one. He looked over at me. "Want it?"

I shook my head 'no' and pulled out a pack I'd bought at County Jail.

His eyes bulged wide. "Tailor-mades?"

I smiled and offered him one, which he gladly accepted, and we both lit up as he told me things the public never hears about why a person is sent to one kind of prison rather than another: how likely he is to escape!

At the top of the heap were places from which it was virtually impossible to break out: behind gun towers manned by officers with loaded rifles, on walls so high that you couldn't jump them and built on soil so impregnated with motion detectors that you couldn't try to crawl out without being noticed. They were called *Level Four* institutions.

Level Three was a place where the soil didn't have those devices, but it still had walls and gun towers with armed guards.

Level Two had a tall chain link fence around it—and, of course, gun towers.

Level One might be a fire fighting camp, up in the forest, with no fence at all. "Just a line you never cross," my cellmate said. And when he saw the look of hunger cross my face, he laughed to himself and added: "Everyone with a long sentence to do starts out at Level Four."

The look vanished.

"Listen," he said. "These people aren't stupid! They know that if you had a chance to do so right now, you'd try to run. So what they do with a new man is put him somewhere at the start of his sentence where he can't possibly escape."

He paused to take another drag from his smoke.

"Later," he went on, "after you've been down a while, they'll move ya. To a less-secure institution, and let you get used to that. And then they'll move you again—in your case, probably a couple of years before you're ready to go home—and in that last place, frankly, you could probably just walk away if you wanted to, it's that casual."

I thought about that for a moment. "Does anyone ever do so?"

He laughed to himself and said, "Nah!"

"Why not?"

"Hell!" he replied, tapping his cigarette over the sink next to his bunk. "The penalty for escape is two years and ya only got two left to do! You've already been down; the worst is behind you; you know you can do the time because you've already done more than two, and you just don't."

He added that there were always a couple of exceptions: "Fools, or guys who just want to get caught and be given more time."

I looked at him, puzzled. "Given more time? Why would anyone want that?"

"Well," he said, looking away from me for a moment, "maybe they ain't got nothin' on the outside."

I couldn't accept that. "But still," I began to say, when he cut me off angrily.

"Look—it's 'three hots and a cot'. Ya get fed three times a day. Ya get a bed to sleep in that's not wet in the wintertime and not crawling with bugs in the summer. Ya get medical care and dental care when you need it. Hell—these eyeglasses I got," and he reached over to pick up a pair resting next to him "—*they* made them for me."

I foolishly asked him how many times he'd been in and he looked away, as if he was staring into his memories.

"Three."

How to Get Help in Prison

I wouldn't see a counselor right away. In the world of prisons no one's in a rush to do anything because, if there's anything an inmate has lots of, it's time and jobs that normally would be done outside in a day took a week to get done here. So I began to wait. The cell was so small and, as there wasn't much room in it to do anything else, I spent most of my time there up on my bunk.

And slept. I began to sleep a lot during the day, so much so that I began to wonder if maybe I could sleep away my whole ten-year sentence. *Maybe I'd just wake up and find the whole thing had only been a dream.*

Other than going to chow three times a day, there was nothing else to do. It got so boring I sometimes went to chow even when I wasn't hungry, and ate anyhow, just for something to do. Einstein was right: time is relative. You can sit down at your computer and knock off some e-mail and be astounded when you find that *two full hours* have just sped by. But when your computer takes sixty seconds to boot-up, it feels like sixty *minutes*!

Prison is like boot-up time. People say: "He *only* did five years." *You* try waiting for your life to boot-up again, for five years!

I finally got to see my intake counselor: a man in his late forties with dark hair and a heavily-lined face, who occupied a small cubicle barely big enough for his desk and a folding metal chair on my side. He sat in one on his side, in his shirtsleeves and tie. My file was in front of him; the one they'd sent over from the court.

"Sit down," he said, when I came to his doorway.

I walked in and did as he said.

He peered down at the file a moment, then looked up and began asking me questions meant to assess what kind of person I was likely to become now, for it would be his job to determine the kind of prison to which I'd be sent. Part of that job was keeping the guards there safe, by not sending them the kind of person with which they usually don't deal, who belongs somewhere else—with other kinds of guards.

He wanted to see if I accepted any responsibility for my crime or if, like many others, I just tried to blame some one else, like my ex-wife or, worse yet, the child. I've seen cases like that: where a nine-year old girl has been sexually abused by her stepfather and he claims it happened because 'she came in while I was in the bathroom,' or similar lame excuses. They're poison in a place like this. Come into prison and tell your intake counselor that it's not your fault and he'll just throw you back into the hopper, to be processed like dog meat.

Similarly, if you come in complaining about the system: "I had a lousy lawyer." Even if it's true, you'd do best to save it for the time when you can file an appeal, not use it as your excuse for being here. Counselors see too many who claim innocence when the record screams out their guilt, and they have a very short fuse for it as they are part of the same team that investigated you and they believe in that team.

If you know anyone who gets convicted of a sex offense—or if you know one of their relatives—and you want them to get help while they're in prison, this is what you tell them: be respectful when you're called in by your first counselor, answering in full and without any excuses every question that you're asked, and express some sense of remorse for what you did that led to your being sent here *for having hurt someone else*!

What the counselor is looking at is your *attitude*. Show a good one, be sincere and truthful, and he can set you on the road to places with resources that will be made available to you as you do your time. Show a bad one, come in whining and complaining—or trying to charm or impress them—and, well, you read about what happens to sex offenders in prisons where they probably shouldn't have been sent but 'mistakes happen,' as they say.

It's up to each prisoner whether they happen to him.

"Never tell anyone what your crime is," my counselor concluded, "or you might get killed for it! Your offense is at the bottom of the criminal hierarchy. When other men ask you what you're in for, say 'embezzlement,' or something like that. Otherwise you won't make it. Many of these men have been sexually molested as kids themselves, or have sisters who were, or kids themselves that they worry about now. They'll take it out on you if they find out why you're here."

He was saving my life, but I couldn't see it at the time. All I could think of was that, if imprisonment is that dangerous, why do they put us here instead of in a mental hospital? What we do isn't a capital offense. Is it just in the *hope* that we'll be killed? My judge had thought that might happen. At the end of pronouncing my sentence, he'd looked across the courtroom at my ex-wife and said, "The child should be told her father is dead!" Now, I receive letters from prisoners in other institutions who say they have the same concerns—and those are what keep them from saying they need help. If they ever got any, everyone would figure out why they, alone, were being seen by a prison psychologist and that would finish them off. So they don't get help and just wait to come back to your society.

We need special yards in prisons, for people like these so they can openly seek treatment, and in some places they're beginning to have them. We need them throughout the prison system.

My counselor stared intensely at me as he ended our interview. "Remember what I said. I'm warning you."

I nodded in agreement, got up and left his tiny cubicle.

The Power of My Life

I lost my cell mate the next day: they shipped him back to the same institution he'd been in before.

He was so *happy* when he got the news!

It was back to waiting until my turn to leave came, back to lying on my bunk all day between meals, with nothing to do and no one to talk to: with nothing but the shredded trappings of a 'self,' and even that soon peeled away. For as I lay there and looked at the ceiling I soon began to see pictures of my life going by like the carved wooden animals on a merry-go-round, from childhood to now, one after another.

They didn't stop. When the cycle reached where I was now, it started all over again. Just when I thought that I'd really go nuts, all of a sudden I saw it: behind these images there was something else—an 'inner projector,' as it were—within my mind that caused them.

My whole life was a projection—*from something else within me!*

I quickly named that something the Power of My Life and knew that it would not abandon me, that this was not to be the way my life ended.

A vision began to appear on the ceiling—of a place at the bottom of a large hill in Hollywood, atop which sat a small temple built by a religious order from India that I used to visit. It was down the street from where I lived, years before, and many an evening I sat on its steps trying to figure myself out during that era when the 'Other' within me was carrying me all over the city on its own nights. The temple's religious order—Vedanta—preached a doctrine demanding that we be who we are, without being attached to the results of our actions while, at the same time, avoiding evil. I never could figure out how to do that, but many a night on its steps there I tried, with all my heart. It's where I began my own quest for timeless answers.

Now, I suddenly realized, this was where my life was going to go. I was going to come back to that spot! Some time, some way, I was going to return there. It was a statement from the Power of My Life that I was going to survive prison. It was a *Promise!*

But would I have any answers by then?

More days of empty waiting followed. In desperation for something else to do—for something to read, just to get my mind off things—I broke line after coming back from chow and bolted through the open doors of the Interfaith Chapel.

Glancing around quickly, I saw what I was looking for, over to one side. On top of a plain wooden table in the corner, there was a whole stack of paperback copies of The Bible.

I snatched one and took it back to my cell. And I began to read it from the very first page.

"In the beginning…"

I read the stories of The Creation, The Flood, of Adam and Eve, Cain and Abel, Noah, Abraham, Isaac and Jacob.

Then I came to *The Story of Joseph*. He, too, had been imprisoned for a sex offense: attempted rape. They'd locked him away for thirteen years.

The charge was false, we're told that, but so what? Thirteen years is a big piece of time, especially when one is young, as Joseph was. He'd only been a kid when he went in—seventeen—the youngest child of jealous older brothers who'd sold him into slavery where he found work in the house of a wealthy man. But the man's wife coveted Joseph and he would not lie with her, for he was loyal to his master. That made the woman spiteful and in her anger she lied and said that Joseph had taken her by force. And down he went into the House of Prison, into his under-world.

But God smiled upon him there and gave him the gift of interpreting dreams, and he soon gained a reputation for doing so among Pharaoh's officials. When the great Pharaoh had dreams that no one else could interpret, it was Joseph for whom they finally sent.

And Joseph interpreted the dreams of Pharaoh, and warned him that, after seven years of plenty that were coming to all of Egypt, there would be seven cruel ones when the land would be gripped by famine, advising Pharaoh to prepare for them by setting aside excess food during the good times. Pharaoh listened to Joseph and appointed him to that task, placing him at his right hand over all others.

The Great Famine came as Joseph predicted, and from all over the region people flocked to Egypt for food, willing to pay any price. Joseph set the price and made Pharaoh even wealthier, and Pharaoh smiled upon Joseph.

One day it was Joseph's older brothers who stood before him to ask for food and they didn't recognize him, for instead of a beardless youth they now faced a fully-bearded man in his thirties, a man of great power and influence second only to that of the Great Pharaoh.

But Joseph recognized them and when he could no longer stand his concealment he broke into tears and revealed himself. They froze in terror. This man could *kill* them merely by nodding to his guards.

Joseph saw their fear and comforted them. "*I am no longer angry for what you did to me when I was a child, for now I know that it was not you— but God, acting through you, who sent me here.*"

Could the answer as to what really causes any tragedy, from avalanches to murders, really be that far away? I've met people who have said so, and seen it comfort them to get past enormous tragedies that have come into their lives. And I've met others who insist that such an idea is mere foolishness, and remain drowning in their own bitterness.

I chose to stand with the first group. I put down *The Bible*, got off my bunk and walked over to my cell door. Gripping its bars with all my strength, I prayed for the first time since I was a child.

"Please! Let it be! Let me too come to know that it was You who sent me here, so I may also come back without hatred for anyone."

Not even for myself.

*   *   *   *   *

Questions for Group Discussion

1. What about life imprisonment, or sentences so long they are equivalent to them? Should criminal sentences include a chance for the person to redeem themselves and come back to the community?

2. Are sex offenses solely the failure of the person committing them, or are they also the failure of the entire tribe? Is our culture too permissive and, therefore, to blame in any way?

3. What advice would you give to a person about to be sent to prison for a sex offense?

4. Is the source of tragedy to be found just in the world and among ourselves? Or are there larger forces that also act? What would you tell a person, to comfort them in the face of enormous personal loss?

5. What would you tell yourself in the same kind of situation? Where would you find your courage?

Chapter Five

Evil or Ill?

From Cure to Control

Treatment for sex offenders is not a new art. In the early part of the twentieth century, neurosurgeons simply cut out that part of the person's brain that had to do with the sex drive. According to Canadian Sex Therapist W.L. Marshall, one of the pioneers of newer treatments, a group of German surgeons were the leading advocates of that earlier method. When they later found that the number of patients who committed new sex crimes following surgery was still no lower than that of those who had been spared the surgeon's knife, the human brain as the sole location of our sex life was dropped, along with that form of therapy.

Surgical castration was popular for awhile in Europe, and at first looked like it promised success as many patients went back to the community and remained arrest-free. But then someone noticed that the patients included a lot of homosexuals, who hadn't raped women or molested children in the first place, which presumably accounted for why they weren't "repeating" those crimes now. When they were removed from the follow-up statistics, early optimism quickly faded as the readjusted figures showed that almost half of all the remaining sex offenders who had been castrated still continued to masturbate or have intercourse.

While a 1968 study indicated that Danish castrates stopped committing any more sex crimes, a third of their number continued to commit other crimes, which suggested that their underlying aggression still hadn't been changed. And when hormones then became commercially available, permitting a patient to nullify the effect of castration, there seemed no point to continue using it, and that method was also discarded.

Psychologists didn't do much better when they applied conventional therapy. One California program for sex offenders had a 19 percent failure rate among its patients over a three year follow-up period. When it was extended to five years, the re-offense rate jumped to 26 percent and the program became politically unsupportable.

The problem, it was later learned, was that therapists were seeking the wrong goal: trying to *cure* a problem that would be more successfully addressed if it was just placed under control. As one leading official in a state mental health department put it:

"...there appears to be an emerging consensus among treatment providers... that the overall goal of treatment is one of management or control, not cure. This rejects the notion that sex offending is an illness from which one will recover and that successful treatment will result in the elimination of the disorder. Instead, it suggests that successful interventions are those that *train offenders to reduce exposure to situations that place them at risk for reoffense...*"

> Marques, et. al, "The Sex Offender Treatment and Evaluation Project, Fourth Report to the Legislature in Response to PC 1365," Division of State Hospitals, Department of Mental Health, October, 1991, p. 5 (Italics added for emphasis.)

A lot of things can't be "cured." No cures exist for AIDS, diabetes, schizophrenia and numerous other medical and psychiatric conditions. But they can be controlled so that the individual afflicted with them can continue to live in the community without endangering himself or anyone else. In spite of the sometimes sensationalistic reporting given the most extreme (and, fortunately, rare) cases, most sex offenders can be taught how to manage their own behavior.

When a new pilot program designed to pursue *self-control* instead of cure was carefully tried out by the State of California, the re-offense rate for its graduates was reduced by two-thirds. Sex offending might not be curable, but it could be controlled—for the rest of the former offender's life—by the offender. According to figures released in 2002, 90% of those who complete treatment do not re-offend, and that is what has made the new therapy worthwhile.

Barriers to Treatment

Treatment doesn't begin until we're ready to really face ourselves. And if you are a *sex offender* in a time when the climate all around the subject has been shaped primarily by the *victims* of sexual offenses, facing yourself may be very hard to do. For victims, quite naturally, choose to utterly demonize sex offenders and they have enormous political influence.

The result, as this chapter will show, is that many of our treatment programs have been hobbled by laws that don't mean to heal anybody, but only seek vengeance.

If, as their sponsors believe, punishment really was the answer, there wouldn't be a sex offender anywhere in the world today! Over the last twenty years, punishment has so reshaped criminal law that penalties have been raised to the skies, yet sex offenders continue to exist and their crimes continue to be as awful as before. Punishment alone, therefore, is not the answer. But it is part of the answer. I know of no better place to put a convicted sex offender than in prison for, like a monastic cell, it leaves him alone with his problems so that he finally has no choice but to face them.

It's punishment *and* treatment, without either dominating the other.

A Certain Kind of Walk

Not long after I saw my counselor at that prison intake facility, I was shackled in chains and put on a prison bus that took me to a penitentiary so new that it still lacked any help whatsoever for anyone: no library, no canteen, no doctors or clinic, nothing. It was one of those new joints: pre-fabricated, with reinforced concrete walls. The walls were bolted together to make buildings inside of which there were two stories of cells on three sides. On the fourth there was a two-storied guards office with a glass-enclosed control booth. The guards spoke to us from inside the control booth through loudspeakers.

The walls around the prison weren't up yet, so it sat under the protection of a ring of gun towers and razor-wire fences that could cut a man in two if he tried to climb over them. There wasn't a tree or even a bush anywhere in sight—either in our yard or beyond those fences—so there was nothing that could hide a man from gunfire if he somehow made it out. They'd removed all of the vegetation before they built the place, leaving the earth as barren as our lives now.

And yet, there was something so subversively *appealing* about it all. Like Death, prison accepts everyone. No one is too bad to be turned away. Or too good. And, once you're in prison, you don't have to *care* anymore. No one expects anything of you, ever again. You can give up, if you want to, and a lot of men do.

I wasn't supposed to have been sent here. My intake counselor had recommended a better place for me, but out of clumsily making a sexual advance on a younger inmate on my tier at the intake facility, other men quickly deduced that I was a child molester. Almost immediately, I found myself facing so much hostility that I had to ask staff for protection and they just put me on the next bus out of there. Now I was at a place that looked like the end of the world.

So that's another lesson that anyone going to prison should learn: *don't become a problem for staff or they'll send you to a place full of nothing but problems.*

I was taken to my new cell by a guard, the door was electronically slid open and I entered carrying my blankets, sheets and a pillow as the door closed behind me. My cellmate was lying back against a pillow on the lower bunk when I came in: a grizzled, older man from a rural background doing a life sentence who'd been in before. He gave me his name and asked me for mine.

But now I felt too ashamed of who I'd been to even want to be him anymore. So I quickly searched within myself for some other name I could use. The memory of my grandfather on my father's side was what came forth—a gentle man who had been the only one in my family who'd ever seemed as if he'd loved me just for being me. And I decided to become him.

"Jake," I said. And I've done my best to honor that name ever since. Soon, I'd also do what many of the other convicts did, and grow a long beard to hide behind, to keep anyone from seeing my face.

To keep me from having to face myself!

My new cellmate got up off his bed and shook my hand heartily. "How much time they give ya, Jake?"

"Ten years," I said.

"A dime!" he exclaimed. "That ain't nothin'. Been down over ten already."

Later, he would point out men who had been in prison two and three times that amount. Now, he opened his shirt pocket and pulled out a pack of cigarettes to offer me one, then lit one for himself. "Whatcha in for?"

"Embezzlement," I replied flatly.

My cellmate said that I'd be given work soon, in the kitchen at first and in a factory later. Those were the only kinds of jobs they had there, and it seemed awfully bleak.

It wasn't long until his prediction came true and I was assigned to the chow hall, working from early in the morning until early in the afternoon. I had the rest of the day to myself, which I used to walk the large oval track around our yard. I walked it to try and get rid of the heavy clouds of depression that had now begun to hang over me. I bowed my head under them as I walked and kept my hands plunged deeply into my pockets. For my life had come to nothing and an ever-hungry regret ate away at me over how I imagined my daughter might wind up, now that I wasn't there to help take care of her. Had I not failed as her father it would not have come to this and I knew it, and that made my pain even worse. That was the beginning of my remorse.

A moment kept coming back to me: it was the moment *after* my ex-wife and her new boyfriend had come over to my place, to get all of my daughter's belongings now that she'd only be living with them. It had been only two days since I had admitted to the child's disclosures. They came to get her clothes, her toys, anything else she had, all of which had been kept in the small bedroom that had been hers in my apartment. Knowing they were arriving, I had everything packed up before they arrived. I did it that morning so I wouldn't have to think about what it would be like when I'd have to face the two of them later that day.

Just as arranged, the two of them showed up, told me they didn't need my help in taking anything down to his car after I offered it to them, and then quickly—and silently—took one box after another. It didn't take long until they were done.

I went back into my daughter's bedroom and looked around after they had gone. It was totally empty now. Nothing was there except a feeling of sadness. That's when it hit me. That's when I realized that I had lost her forever. It was in that moment that I collapsed onto the floor and buried my face into the deep pile carpet as a wail of pain broke right on through me.

That was the pain that continued to hang over me now and I quickly found I couldn't escape from it, whether through walking the prison yard, retreating into my dreams at night or even in watching TV.

At 4 o'clock every day, we all had to get back into our cells to be counted, so the prison could be sure that no one had escaped. Men who had them were allowed to watch their small television sets, and my cellmate always turned on his. There was nothing but talk shows everyday, and every talk show that year seemed to focus on nothing but sexual misconduct, especially within the family.

Having to listen to that was like hearing two angry cats clawing at each other inside of me. I wanted to scream at my cellmate to turn it off, but I couldn't say a thing as my counselor's advice continually replayed itself in my mind: "Never tell anyone what your crime is or you might get killed for it."

My pain followed me into the night, where I dreamed troublesome dreams that often woke me up.

So I walked the Yard every day, in mourning for my life, and it wasn't long until some of the men began taking bets on how soon I'd hang myself in my cell. For they'd seen other men take that same kind of walk before and they knew where it led.

It surely would have but, after I'd been there just over four months, my sentence automatically came up for reconsideration by the court and knowing that it would was what kept me alive. They shipped me back to

County Jail for the hearing and I hoped with all my heart that the court might change my sentence to one of probation, allowing me to go free under supervision in the community. But a few days before my case was to be heard, I was told that wasn't likely to happen. A friend of mine had spoken to the judge on my behalf and now came to see me.

"He wants you to do hard time," she told me, assessing what he had said to her in chambers. My nerves cracked under the pressure, and that night I began to hear voices urging me to kill myself. I fought with them until I realized that, before the night was over, they were going to win.

"Deputy!" I called out fearfully.

One responded right away and I broke down crying as I described what was going on within me.

Staff immediately moved me into the County Jail's mental health ward, where I was given medication. As soon as I was stabilized enough, I was taken to court and my case was heard.

The hearing was as brief as it was unrewarding. The Judge said he had reviewed the report he had requested from prison officials as to how I was doing and they had rated me as *adjusting satisfactorily*.

"I see no reason to disturb the sentence."

I was sent back to my penitentiary, but because of that near-suicidal episode, transferred to a nearby prison medical facility where I finally began to get help. I was ready for it now and I welcomed it.

Can Sex Offenders Help Sex Offenders?

All my life, I had been driven by a compulsion to chase after teenage boys. Now, for reasons I wasn't even remotely able to understand, I had also been driven to harm my daughter. What might I be driven to do next? How could I possibly hope to have a life unless I got whatever it was that was crazy in me totally under control?

I put in a request to see a psychotherapist and it was granted. I was sent to see a psychologist who told me she had formerly treated the child victims of sexual abuse and now sought to treat men like me so that none of us would ever harm another child again. Once a week, she permitted many of us under her care to meet among ourselves in a nearby conference room where we were allowed to run our own therapy group.

"I can't get you into it," she told me. "That's up to the men. But I can nominate you for their consideration and you'll be summoned to appear before them. If you can convince them that you belong in their group, they'll admit you as a member. It's up to you."

She said that what they'd insist upon most is total honesty on my part. There'd be no admittance if I tried to deny my crimes, or place their responsibility on anyone else but myself.

I asked her to put my name forth and a week later I was called to their meeting. Upon entering, I found a dozen men seated on both sides of a long conference table: rapists, child molesters, sex offenders of every kind, maybe even killers. Instantly I knew that, if I tried to lie about anything, it wouldn't work—for these men had probably told the same lies and would see right through me.

A man that I'll call William was their chairman: a fiftyish man with a gray Van Dyke beard who sat in a perfectly starched-and-ironed sky-blue prison shirt and brand-new dark blue jeans at the far end of table. With clothes like that, obviously, he had juice in this prison and knew how to get things done. I could see why he was the chairman.

He was smoking a pipe as I came in and took it out as he smiled and said: "Welcome to our group."

I stood at my end of the table. "Thank you."

"Why don't you tell us what you were convicted for?"

"I molested my daughter, several times."

One of the men asked, "Do you take responsibility for what you did?"

"I do."

Then the questions began to come at me from all of the others, hard and fast.

"Why did you do it?

"Did you ever consider the damage you were causing her?"

"Why didn't you seek professional help?"

And, finally, the most difficult question of all: "Why didn't you stop?"

Snapshot memories flickered past in my mind, leaving painful after-trails.

"Why didn't you stop? Tell us!"

All of my accumulated pain was about to come down.

"A part of me was too angry to stop," I tried to explain.

But the men weren't buying it and tears began to stream down my face as I quickly amended my answer.

"I was too weak to protect her—*from myself!*"

The pain fell on me like an avalanche. Instantly, I covered my face with my hands as I sobbed into them. "And I'm so very *ashamed* of myself!"

Somebody handed me a nearby box of facial tissues and moments later I was quietly asked to wait outside while the members balloted among themselves. I thought I'd seen tears in the eyes of a couple of the other men as I left, but I couldn't be sure. When the door was opened again, I walked back in and returned to my end of the table to wait as William recited the group's decision.

"We decline to accept you."

It was like a blow to the pit of my stomach, but I held it in and politely responded, "That is your right and I accept it. Thank you for considering me."

I turned to leave and grasped the doorknob.

"Wait!"

It was William's voice. When I turned around to face him, all of the men were smiling at me now.

"That was the last test," he said, gently. "We give it to all the men, to make sure they'll accept our authority. We welcome you—as our newest member."

I was in!

With their help, I soon learned that sexual misconduct is the final product of a chain of mental events. The first link in that chain is an *impulse* that ripens into an *idea* and finally becomes an *action*. Impulses are harmless, everyone has them. A man sees a pretty girl and, instantly, has a sexual impulse toward her. But, since it's only an impulse, his reasoning mind steps in and restrains him from doing anything about it, so the impulse evaporates and he goes on with his life as if the impulse had never occurred.

In a sex offender that doesn't happen. Instead, the impulse becomes an idea so alluring that he falls under its spell and the act results. He becomes drawn to act by the hypnotic nature of the idea his own mind has formed.

As I learned from these men, the earlier we choose to halt this process, the easier it is to do so. *Impulses* can be escaped. A man can make himself start thinking of something else that's much healthier for him. If he doesn't, and allows it to become an *idea*, he's in danger, and so is his potential victim. For now, the impulse is gathering strength and soon will be harder to stop.

We called this process our Chain of Causes, with each one leading to the next. Breaking that chain—the sooner, the better—became our motto. We meant to take back control of our mind by assuming responsibility for what we allowed it to do.

Thanks to my therapist, I soon gave up the hope that I had been cherishing of reuniting with my daughter after I got back from prison. I had mentioned it at one of my sessions with the doctor and she helped me to see that it was only a nice daydream I was having.

"Look," she said, gently. "When you get out, your daughter is going to be in adolescence. Do you really think that a young girl at that sensitive stage of her life is really going to want a father around who has just gotten out of prison for doing what you did?"

Even I could see what she meant.

My therapist suggested, instead, that it might be much better if I wrote a short note to my daughter right then, letting her know that I still loved her, but saying a final 'good-bye.' Since Christmas was approaching, she suggested I buy a nice card in the prison store, volunteering to mail it for me.

"Keep the note short," she said.

I followed her advice.

Twelve Step Programs

The teachings of *Alcoholics Anonymous* also helped me. I was given library privileges and, the first day I went there, I found a book published by that organization that spoke right to me. They used a method called the Twelve

Step Program that began with an admission that one's life was out of control, and destructive.

I was able to admit that.

They went on to suggest that we all have some *Higher Power* to which we can turn to help us place our life back under control. That higher power could be God, or one's center of consciousness, or anything else a person finds that has a greater power than him. For some who aren't at all religious, *the group* in Alcoholics Anonymous becomes their higher power.

Having already had that shattering experience with the *I Ching* on sentencing day, when it accurately foretold my imprisonment, I certainly believed now that higher powers existed. And, as a result, what Alcoholics Anonymous was talking about made perfect sense to me. The only problem was that, since I wasn't an alcoholic, I wasn't sure their methods would work for me.

But that was just then. As I would learn, the same methods used by Alcoholics Anonymous have now been adapted for successful use with addicts of all kinds: from compulsive gamblers to narcotics users. Not much before my discovery of AA's book, several sexual compulsives in the United States had already started using their own adaptation of this program to tame themselves. Since then, over half a dozen national and worldwide organizations that help anyone struggling with what are usually less serious sexual problems—such as excessive masturbation, compulsive purchases of pornography or compulsive visits to prostitutes—use a similar adaptation. (See: **Self Recovery Organizations** in the Readers Resources section of this book.)

Not only that, but many government mental health programs for serious sex offenders include an approach similar to AA's within their own spectrum of therapies.

This is not to say that all sexual offenders are merely *sex addicts* who can place their urges under voluntary control. Where a sexual offense includes severe physical violence or is based upon urges too strong to be overcome by AA's Twelve Step Method, deeper therapies have to be used that often require their recipient to be kept within a secure facility over an extended period of time. Or given chemical means to suppress his sexual urges (chemical castration). But, for many of us, the Twelve Step approach is one that helps and, as I would soon find out, it would help me, too.

Human After All

Several months later I was transferred to another prison, a *protective custody* facility for the state's most vulnerable prisoners: people who would be killed or ruthlessly victimized by other prisoners in any other penal institution. Among its inhabitants could be found convicted judges, cops, prosecutors; gang dropouts who had left their criminal organizations by "cooperating" with the authorities in return for a lighter sentence, inmates so emotionally impaired they would be preyed upon endlessly at a regular prison, sex offenders, and—in a separate yard—younger prisoners who looked too pretty for their own safety and would be raped until they committed suicide anywhere else.

It was 'live and let live' here. Nobody made any trouble, for they knew that, if they did, they would be transferred to a regular facility and, as a result, everybody *got along*.

Because of my law background, I was immediately invited by one of the more influential prisoners on the yard to become his cellmate in exchange for helping him with his appeal. A large Italian man who liked to eat, his cell had shelves built on to the walls that held every kind of food sold by the prison canteen, and he generously shared everything he had.

As I worked on his case, we got to know each other. One night, I told him why I had really been sent to prison, but changed the story some to make it look as if I'd been framed by my ex-wife.

That was a big mistake, for word got around and, two days later, someone approached me on the yard and said that I could have her killed, just because she had framed me.

I suddenly realized what I had almost done. That night, I corrected it by telling my cellmate the truth: that the charges brought against me had been completely deserved, that I had molested my own daughter. It was just after lights out, and he was lying on his side on the upper bunk.

He leaned over and looked down at me. "You poor lost soul," he said, quietly. "You poor, poor lost soul."

That was when I began to suspect how very far into the darkness I had gone.

Was I the *worst* of such men? I had to know and, as there were so many of us here—where it was safe to talk among ourselves—I went out into the prison yard to meet some of my peers so that I could measure myself against them. The first thing I learned is that, as Sex Offender Psychologist Anna C. Salter writes, there are two kinds of sex offenders:

- The Opportunists, who really aren't sex offenders as much as people with weak morals who merely find themselves in a tempting situation and take advantage of it, like the burglar who happens to break into the apartment of a young, attractive woman, and then decides to rape her, and

- The Compulsives, people who act out because of an inner urge they haven't yet learned how to control.

The second thing I learned is why some sex offenders in prison don't choose to reform. They don't think that anything is *wrong* with them.

There was the Satanist who had been convicted of ritually killing a 14-year old boy. A bulky man in his thirties, with a dark little beard and *very* dark eyes, he confided that, "*Satan made me do it! He promised that, if I'd do it, he'd always be with me!*"

Presumably for life without the possibility of parole, for that's what he got.

There was the child molester who stalked little girls until he knew where they lived and when they were home alone. The next time they were alone, he'd knock at their door, telling the child he was from the "health" department and needed to examine her.

He told me he was caught when the father of one of the children returned early.

"He grabbed a butcher knife and tried to kill me!"

Terrified, he ran out of the apartment house, with the outraged father in hot pursuit, angrily wielding the huge knife.

Just as he reached the street, a black-and-white police car happened to round the corner and the molester plunged in its way and stopped it.

"I did it!" he told them. "Take me in!"

They did: for twenty years.

Twice I was later celled with rapists. One had committed his crime while the woman's little daughter was in the same room and looked on in shock. He said that he still thought the child's being there was just *funny, like a joke.*

The other was even more menacing. When he found that I was reading books on boating, a popular fantasy interest for many inmates, he asked me if you can "rent" a boat.

"Certainly," I said, putting down the book to look at him. He was in his late twenties, with a trim build and light brown hair; someone who would be attractive to many women.

A snarl could be heard in his voice as he exclaimed, "That's what I'm going to do when I get out of here: rent myself a boat, on some lake, and take some *bitch* out on it, *and rape the fuck out of her!*"

I'm sure he meant it.

Then there was the self-educated intellectual who simply insisted that he had a *natural right* to go after what he called *Little Lolitas*. Bespectacled and in his fifties, he said, "There have always been sexual relations between some adults and children, everywhere in the world, and there always will be. People don't have to be limited to having sex just with other adults. Sexual pleasure isn't just one note, but a whole chorus of them."

It was his argument that the only thing that made sex a *crime* was the country in which it took place, and there is some truth to that. According to one study, rape is only rape when a man does it in some countries and the victim is a woman. In other countries, if the victim is a boy, that's not so. Similarly, unless the child is under Age 16 in some European countries, Age 15 in others, 14 in yet others and 12 in Spain, the crime of child sex abuse hasn't been committed!

And not all countries punish sex offenses with equal severity. In one European country, a sin of the flesh can draw a fine of just under five U.S. dollars while, in a neighboring state, the same one is worth $146,790.11.

Anxious to win me to his side, he urged me to read the man he considered his champion, French intellectual Michel Foucault, one of that country's most celebrated thinkers. "He explains why we have the sexual rules we live by today."

I did so. I got a hold of Foucault's *The History of Sexuality, Volume I,* which argues that sexual restraint is the result of capitalism's need to commercialize everything, making people pay for what they formerly had for free. In the author's "repressive hypothesis", he says that sex didn't become a police matter until the Sovereign realized that population is the source of wealth: hence, the more people, the more workers; causing any sexual practice that didn't result in reproduction to suddenly be called a *deviance.*

From my friend's viewpoint, the only basis for morality is economics—when, in fact, morals are really another name for our values. Like them, they're absolutely fundamental to who we are as a people. But that's not always so easy to accept when you've spent a lifetime living in the grip of urges that lead you to ignore morals.

Out of my talks with this man, however, what I finally realized was that there have always been men (and women) like us and, presumably, always will be. We are a recurrent sexual direction that has appeared in virtually every group of people that has ever existed. What that suggests is that there always will be people like us in every generation. We are not just today's departure from the norm. We have always been and always will be something beyond the norm. We are part of what it means to say there is a *human* species, hard as that may be to accept.

As I discovered in prison among these men, our backgrounds are very common, and our mothers so much like each other that we even joked among ourselves that any one of us could get on a pay phone with someone else's mother and not even notice the difference.

Nor, probably, would she.

Tremendously possessive, they smothered us and in the process sought to devour us. Always treating us as if we were children, they stunted our growth by always making an excuse for us whenever we failed. And that made me wonder just how safe our mothers would be, if we got involved with them again or let them get involved in our lives, when we got out—as most such men did, for no one else would take them.

To Heal or To Punish?

When my request for further psychotherapy was approved, I was given a prison psychologist with whom I'd meet each Monday for one hour. To prepare for those sessions, I had the guards lock me in my cell alone the day beforehand, so I could have the time and the privacy to search within myself for anything I wanted to bring up. More than anything, I wanted to know why I had lost control with my daughter as my whole history had been only with boys in their teens. I had to understand what was so out of control within me for I feared that, if I didn't, I couldn't be sure what it would lead me to do next.

I was amazed to find so many injuries buried in my memories: things like the fact that my father had rejected me as a child, for not liking football or baseball, like he did. I liked swimming and, when I got into my teens, I'd even begun working-out at a gym, but those weren't good enough to earn his acceptance and that hurt me, even then.

Then there was my mother, and all those times when she'd kept me from being *me* by denying that I felt whatever I felt if it differed at all from how she felt.

What I soon realized was that, like all sex offenders, I'd never really had any sense of self and, hence, no self-*respect*. Lacking that, I'd been unable to respect anybody else. The lesson that leaves us with is that, if you want your child to become a moral person, you begin by respecting him or her as a person.

I told my doctor that the specific reason I wanted to see him was because I wanted to learn why I had molested my daughter. Fearful that I might be prosecuted further if I said anything about any other acts I had committed, I did what everyone else did in prison and never mentioned them. Had I done otherwise, they would have been reported and I might have had to face additional charges.

Some say that not talking about them is harmful, as it doesn't get all of the person's problems addressed. In a case handed down in the United States just before the time of this writing (*McKune v. Lile*), the Supreme Court said much the same thing and gave states permission to make a prisoner's confinement even *harsher* if he wouldn't also tell them about crimes for which he had not yet been caught. But doctors I know who conduct group therapy programs outside of prison, which often include men still awaiting trial—who can't talk about their crimes, on the advice of their attorney—say that such men are still dealing with their problems, just by being in the group. "They hear what we're saying and know if it applies to them."

Perhaps what the defense bar still hasn't succeeded in communicating to the bench is that, unlike tent revival meetings, where a sinner cannot be forgiven unless he loudly proclaims all his sins to others—a hallowed proceeding in recent Western history and still a very popular vehicle in some places—psychotherapy is a different kind of process altogether. What is necessary here is that you face the truth about yourself—*to yourself.*

The fact is that it is the individual in therapy who has to do the work, not the doctor. Whether the client tells the doctor about something or not, the client still knows what that something is and is working on it, even when confining the discussion only to those things which can safely be discussed.

As I wrote, in part, to *The New York Times* reporter who covered that United States Supreme Court case:

> For all the importance that an honest admission has, speaking out of my own experience I say that it doesn't necessarily have to be made to a person who will prosecute you for it…
>
> There are those who, as in *Lile*, believe…one can only find redemption by self-rejection, while there are others…who believe one can only find redemption by accepting one's self as their life does: as a work still in progress, and then progressing it.
>
> —*E-mail to Linda Greenhouse dated January 11, 2002*

Who is going to risk being given another prison sentence when they haven't even finished the one they already have, just to fill-in the record?

To meet this challenge, some prosecutors are now choosing not to press charges for disclosures made by prisoners in prison therapy programs. They are issuing what are called *waivers* from further prosecution for anything admitted in counseling, and that's helping a lot of men get the help they need without having to fear more jail time for doing so.

The only problem is that further prosecution isn't the only threat that an admitted offender now faces. Since at least the early nineties in the United States, new laws require many sex offenders to be committed to mental hospitals *after* their imprisonment if they admit to having had two or more victims, keeping them locked up even longer. As a result, some defense attorneys are warning their clients that freedom from prosecution isn't enough and, so far as this writer knows, no prosecutor yet has waived both further prosecution *and* post-imprisonment civil commitment, moving us right back to where we started: offenders—fearful of no end to being kept locked up—are not willing to divulge any other crimes than the ones for which they've been convicted.

As a result, many of them are coming back out on the streets without *any* treatment in many instances.

Blame and Responsibility

My doctor was no fool, by the way. He was a *prison* psychologist, used to facing men who lied to him every day. I doubt if I really had to tell him there might have been other offenses. As a result, by the end of a year of our meeting together, he had some answers for me.

"While it's clear that your father never molested you, there's no question but that he was, shall we say, 'overly-affectionate.' And that it was your mother who was the problem."

I recall that he said I should *hate* her "as she was the one who messed you up."

He wasn't the only doctor who had said so. While my case was waiting to be heard and I was in treatment then, another doctor had said the same thing.

But as I told the doctor I had now, I just didn't think that hating my mother was the answer.

"I know too much about her own background to do that. That she damaged me I do not doubt. But that she *alone* did so is untrue as she, in turn, had been damaged by those who raised her who, in turn, had been damaged by others, and so on, making it merely an act of choice to say we shall *blame* her, as if none of these others had ever existed."

Blame is just a *legal* term, used by courts to determine who is going to pay the injured party, in cash or through involuntary servitude as a prisoner of the state. It has nothing to do with therapy or healing, where what we can do is identify where the damage came from so that we can heal it or at least get away from it.

Other people who look like the creator of the damage are really only *carriers* of a damaging process that moves through them. While they can be held *accountable* for letting it come through—and should be—we can't accurately call anyone it's *real* creator because there is no such individual. There is just life, and in life sometimes people get hurt: earthquakes happen and people get injured by them. Emotional earthquakes happen too, and that's what sometimes makes a parent fail. You can't *blame* anyone for having an emotional earthquake. You can build them back up so they don't have another.

In that respect, the view expressed by our criminal law—that the offender, alone, is to blame for having become an offender—is like blaming the rain on itself, without including the climate that produced it. In the victim's pain, he or she wants vengeance, and who can fault them? In their pain, all they can see is the person standing in the dock, not all the others who may go back for generations in the forming of the offender. And so the victim cries out of their pain: "Punish him!"

But law should have more vision than that and, instead of merely punishing, it should seek to confine the offender in prison until he is healed, and see that they get an opportunity to be healed: that would be wisdom, which we have a right to demand of the law.

The doctor stared at me in wonder, and with a wry grin on his face said, "You're crazy, did you know that? You're as crazy as (the craziest inmate he could think of)."

I wanted additional answers, so the following week I sent in a request for something called *transpersonal counseling*, which would look not only at my mind but into my spirit itself, for I now suspected that this had been damaged within me too, and needed to be fixed if I was ever to have a life that was under control. When I received a reply that this kind of counseling wasn't available in any of the prison's psychology programs I turned, instead, to where it could be found: in the Chaplain's Office.

Just before I did so, a notorious child molester died on our tier. He had been in the television room, having sex with one of the younger inmates in a back row when he had a heart attack. Everyone was locked in their cells afterwards and I stood peering out the small window set at eye-level in my door when they brought his body past on a stretcher. All of the men did the same, and taunted him as he came by, including those who had used him for sexual relief themselves:

"Go to Hell, faggot!"

"You finally got what's comin', you dirty old Queer!"

"Goodbye, man: give your peter to Saint Peter!"

I barely knew the man by name, yet all I could do was weep as he went by, knowing that's what awaited me too…if I failed to change myself now.

Since that time, therapy programs available to convicted sex offenders in many places have become even richer than the ones that were made available to me. Developed primarily in Canada, they provide tools to clinicians using them that help offenders understand their own perception of other people as sexual objects is an actual *distortion* in the way the mind works, and one that can be corrected.

There are role-playing therapies that let us experience what it feels like to be a victim; empathy therapy that lets us feel what someone else feels; drugs to control deviant sexual fantasies that would otherwise overpower us; reconditioning therapies that let us substitute more normal urges for the ones we formerly followed.

Among even newer additions, there's biofeedback training that teaches us how we can alter our internal states to reduce or even eliminate the need for any medication to control our minds. There are even therapies to provide us with the social skills training that so many of us lack, which used to keep us from being able to have more normal relationships.

They can now teach us how to become a *person* instead of just a carrier of a sexual urge.

They should do so everywhere and, if you speak out, they would.

*   *   *

Questions for Group Discussion

1. What do you think of the idea of having convicted sex offenders conducting counseling groups for newer offenders?
2. Is sex an urge, an impulse or a deliberate choice?
3. If you were a convicted sex offender, would you admit to every crime you committed, including the ones for which you had not yet been caught?
4. Is the sex offender less blameworthy if he was molested himself as a child?
5. Is the parent who damages their child to be blamed for how that child turns out? Or is there a line somewhere, when we can say they are excused and only their child is accountable?

Chapter Six

Wrestling With The Sexual Self

Can religion 'save' a sex offender? One of the convicted predators I met there—who had now become a very devout Catholic—told me that he knew he would never offend again when he got out as "Jesus" would save him.

I question whether we have the right to make that job His. In recovery literature, there's an anonymous saying I like much better: "*Without God, I can't. Without me, God won't.*"

It's neither fair nor reasonable that we look for miracles to save us, although, of course, they might. What I've found more likely is that being religious can empower our journey into recovery by making it a *spiritual* quest, too. We need the spiritual dimension in this work for, only too often, as I've attempted to show so far, we're already in its dark side.

I was fortunate. A full-time Jewish chaplain had just been added to the staff of our institution and I seized that opportunity to place myself under his teaching. In his forties and thin as a rail, with a small prayer cap always worn on top of his head, he squinted at me from behind rimless eyeglasses as I told him, "I'd like to study Jewish Mysticism."

His reply was unconditional. "I don't teach *Jewish Mysticism*."

I nodded that I understood, for mysticism—in any religion—doesn't just deal with knowing about the *Almighty* but directly experiencing it in your life, which is not a light thing to take on. But if I really wanted to fix myself, I knew this was the level I'd have to reach.

Seeing the determined look on my face he added, "But I'll tell you what I will do. If you will let me teach you the fundamentals of our religion, after I'm done—if you still want to study 'Jewish Mysticism'—I'll get you some scholarly books on the subject and you can study it yourself."

He warned me that 'mysticism'—and mystic experiences—can be very taxing. "Our state mental hospitals," he cautioned me, "are just full of 'Great Jewish Mystics' and I don't want you to become another one. But if you have your fundamentals and ever get lost out there, at least you'll have a safety net to fall back on."

That seemed perfectly reasonable and I accepted his conditions. Whenever I wasn't working at a prison-assigned job, I studied the materials he gave me to use in my cell and then went to see him once each week to discuss them.

A Yeshiva Behind Bars

We began with a basic primer, and then went on to study the Holy Scriptures (what non-Jews call "The Old Testament"). Under his guidance, what I found repeatedly was a *call* within them throughout the darkness of eternity from a parent who ached for the return of a child who called back that it was lost. What I came to see is that humanity needs God to find itself just as much as God needs humanity to know itself.

When I learned enough Hebrew to do so, I went on to study *Torah*, the sacred writings of our people. The word means "plan" and its central concept is that there is a plan for our lives and that *Torah* contains that plan in symbolic form. The work contains the first five books of the Old Testament. Originally written on long sections of sheepskin called *sedras*, one section is read every week on the Sabbath: to mirror the changing phases of the Moon that mirror the changing phases of our lives. All of these *sedras* were sewn together, end-upon-end, and then suspended between two long spools upon which they could be rolled. Each week, when *Torah* is brought out, it's unrolled, just like our destiny.

Collectively, the story it tells is one of estrangement and reconciliation: creation, fall from grace, a life that's flooded and then recovers, only to wind up becoming enslaved before one's worthiness is tested and one's Promised Land is finally found.

The Rabbi was very specific about that enslavement. "It wasn't just to Egypt," he insisted, referring to the story found in The Book of Exodus.

"It's enslavement to the *world*. You can get just as enslaved today by having too much credit card debt, or by living a life so secular that it doesn't include any lasting values. *Torah* tells us that our people came to be so dominated by the world of their time that they couldn't even *remember* the name of their God."

I saw the truth of what he was saying in my own life.

"That's when you're really lost," he concluded. Embarrassed, I cleared my throat.

We went beyond Judaism, into the time before there was a Judaism, back before the time of Moses. It can be found in the Book of Genesis, where one reads of a people called the *Ha-biru* (later known as: Hebrews) which means: the one's from "the other side" of the city walls, the peoples of the Sinai Desert who at one time worshipped a Goddess named Sin (pronounced *Seen*). It is said that her symbol was The Moon for, just like life, the Moon is always changing on its surface while its wholeness remains constant. She was said to have presided over her holy desert in which they lived, from atop her sacred mountain where she watched them dance out their lives below. Hence, both were named after her: Mount *Sin*-ai and the *Sin*-ai Desert.

Her legacy remains today in the Jewish Mystical notion of the *Shekinah*, or Bride of God, the feminine side of the Godhead, to whom a glass of wine is raised—just like one does at weddings—on every sabbath coinciding with the New Moon. Every Jewish man is potentially her groom and every Jewish woman represents The Bride of God.

And that's when the Rabbi directed his teaching to my case.

"Tell me," he said, leaning back in the chair behind his desk, "do you have any idea why we consecrate our allegiance to God by placing the Mark of Circumcision on *that* particular part of the human body?

"No," I said, completely puzzled. I'd never thought about it before.

"Well," he responded, "think about it. I mean, we could have placed such a mark elsewhere, by notching our ears, or nose, as other peoples have done. Why do you think we chose to make that mark on the *penis?*"

I squirmed in my seat as I said that I couldn't imagine a reason why. Then he gave me the answer. "We put it there," he told me sternly, "to remind ourselves that *all* of our urges must be submitted to the Will of God—even *that* one."

A wall of shame fell over me. I had not just sinned against the law, but against the Giver of Law.

That night, alone in my cell, with the moon as my only witness through the barred window, I got down on my knees on the smoothly polished concrete floor, bowed my head and made my confession.

"Aveinu malkeno," I began aloud, in Hebrew.

I was offering what is called *The Midnight Prayer*: one that cannot be heard until one reaches the midnight of their life as it cannot be spoken until it is midnight in one's soul.

"My father, my king: forgive me, for I have *offended* Thee…"

There is a Plan.

Conversations with Divinity

True to his word, once I'd satisfied him that I'd mastered all of Judaism's essentials, the Rabbi supplied me with several of the finest works on Jewish Mysticism and I spent the balance of my tutorial under him in studying them. My conclusions are my own, however, and should not be taken as his, for the essence of mysticism is what it is for you-only (which every religious fanatic either forgets or never understands).

What I came to see is that Judaism is rooted in the notion of a future we are permitted to help form *by knowing it in advance.* Not only was our religion founded by an astrologer (Abraham, who—after casting his own horoscope—is said to have exclaimed, "There is a Plan; hence, there must be a Planner.") but in the first book of the Bible we are told of a man who could tell the future from dreams (Joseph). In other portions of the Bible we are given accounts of at least *eighteen* major prophets, all of whom foretold what was to happen.

In addition, I found that when the Hebrew people made their way across the Sinai Desert to go to the Promised Land, they did so using a divinatory device called the *ephod.* From the time of *Exodus* on, we are told it was worn by the high priest, over which a breast piece was placed that had a pouch or pocket in which two small flat or rounded objects were kept which were cast as lots to *divine God's will* (just as many Christians have long since done by turning to the Bible for advice, by opening it at random and reading whatever it says there).

King David wore an *ephod* and its divinatory functions were enlisted by him on at least two occasions: to learn his own fate against Saul and escape it (which he did, thanks to the reply he received) and to recover his two wives and the daughters of his countrymen who had been carried away by the Amalekites (1 Sam.23:9; 30:7, respectively). The prophet Michah is believed to have worn the *ephod* in his role as a diviner, as did Samuel while ministering at Shiloh (1 Sam. 2:18).

According to *Erdman's Bible Dictionary* (1987), the *ephod* "is at times clearly linked with eliciting an *oracle...*" (Italics added for emphasis.)

"That doesn't make us puppets," the Rabbi told me. "The fact that God knows what we're going to do and can tell others in advance doesn't mean that we don't make the choice."

Judaism speaks of a *yetzer*, or inclination, that we have: one for good and one for evil. "Cain," the Rabbi reminded me, "was warned by God just before Cain slew his brother: 'Your evil *inclination* lies at your door. This is your chance to subdue it.' Cain had free will and so do we."

From what I could see, the original promise of Judaism is that, while we are given the *conditions* of our lives—where we are born, who our parents are, things like that—*how* we use those conditions is up to us. Thus, we are neither puppet *nor* sole author of our lives, but *co*-author with their Creator.

According to scholarly sources, the *ephod* disappeared from the High Temple following the Babylonian Conquest. But there are other instruments of sacred divination still available to humanity and one of the oldest and most revered has been preserved by the Chinese, in their classic work, *I Ching*. By this time, I had two translations of that work which I'd purchased from their publishers, and the books were in my cell where I was studying them. For the *I Ching*, too, sets forth a Plan not much different than that of *Torah*.

Doing Time with the *I Ching*

Originally transmitted only by memory, 3000 years ago the work was first written down: by a prisoner. He was later known by the name of King Wen and led a revolt against the ruling dynasty in China. Captured by his enemies, he was locked up and held for ransom. It was during his imprisonment that he produced the first written version of this work. When his son later rescued him, they completed the revolution and founded what became known as the Chou Dynasty. The *I Ching* then became the official bible of their kingdom. When the great Chinese philosopher, Confucius, later added explanations to the writings that King Wen left us, the work went on to become the most revered book in Chinese literature.

The *I Ching*, too, issues a call: to live a balanced life in harmony with everything around you. Out of studying this work, what I learned is that it is the normal course of our lives to be filled and then emptied, *repeatedly*. When I finally grasped this completely, it totally changed the way I saw the world and that's when my recovery took root.

I remember the very moment. I'd just flashed my pass in front of a video camera by a gate, to go from one yard to another, on an errand for one of the prison's officials. When the gateway opened wide, I suddenly understood the *I Ching*'s idea in full: *All creation is in opposites!* You can't have any kind of experience in this world without also having its opposite. If you have *good* in your life, it then drains away and some bad always flows in, just to balance it. As sunrise always leads to sunset, pleasure always leads to pain.

It's unavoidable. One can no more have 'good' without 'bad' than one can take just half a breath. You always get both. Those are the tides of life and the person who understands this doesn't seek to climb every peak that is possible, for he or she knows that on the other side there is nowhere to go but down. One walks a modest path instead and is left in relative peace.

That's when I realized that, in accordance with that law, if I ever again sought another experience of overly-intense sexual pleasure—and that's what all forbidden sex is—an overly-intense *un*pleasant experience would always follow.

It might be jail. It might be a sexually-transmitted disease. It might be the fear of jail, so great that I'd always be on the run, always worried that, someday, they might catch me. It might be revenge, cruelly taken by someone on behalf of the person I had molested.

It isn't just a matter of what society's law says. Any reasonably intelligent person can figure out a way to evade that, at least for awhile, or go live in some other country where the laws aren't so strict. But what this teaching was telling me was that there is *another* law, like gravity: so sewn into the very fabric of life that, no matter where I ran and what I did, it would be impossible for me to keep from experiencing it.

Everything has consequences, and those consequences will come down on us, no matter where we are. All we can change is *where* they will find us, not whether. We're not looking at a law of society's. We're looking at a *law of life*.

No wonder I wound up being sent to prison! I had invoked it, just by the kind of life I had lived. I could no more harm another without harming myself than I could take a hammer and hit my own toe without feeling pain. The victim of an act of sexual abuse isn't the only one injured by it: so is the offender and, the sooner the offender realizes this, the sooner he will stop being an offender. It is inescapable.

The dark lord of my life had just been dethroned!

The Lessons of Imprisonment

Other lessons soon followed.

I went to the prison library and brought books back to my cell that let me read about other men's imprisonment, in other lands and at other times, so that I could better understand my own. For imprisonment, no matter when it is and where it is, always has something about it at its core that makes it uniformly the same, as if one has entered a timeless *brotherhood* that cuts right across centuries and civilizations and somehow unites them.

I read about Japanese internment camps in the Pacific, for civilians unfortunate enough to have been placed in them. I read Solzhenitsyns' massive work, *The Gulag Archipelago*, which described the brutality of the former Soviet Union's prison camps in Siberia during the 1930's and 1940's. I read about Nazi concentration camps and the experiences of Jews who had lived in them during World War II. All of these books taught me something.

Solzhenitsyn wrote that evil has what he called a *threshold magnitude*— a point which, once passed, makes it impossible for a person to ever come back to the human campfire because he has gone so far into the darkness that there isn't time enough in a human life to make the return journey.

I wondered, in fear, if this might apply to me, but decided that, while a person might commit an act so evil that they would never be welcome back in mainstream society, he could still come back from evil and live a better life, even if outside of society or on its margins. In former times, we had the French Foreign Legion, where such men were posted in distant lands, given new names and never heard of again, while serving their country's interests. In even earlier times we had the monastery. Finding their equivalent is the challenge now, and they're there, if in no other place than working as a *street counselor* for a community corrections agency. Anyone can redeem themselves, if they want to do so enough, as the rite of redemption is given by the nature of life itself.

I read Elie Wiesel's poignant story of the time when everyone in his Nazi concentration camp was made to silently witness the hanging of three of its members suspected of being saboteurs, one of whom was only a child.

He tells us that members of the SS placed a noose around the little boy's neck just like they had done with the others. The two adults died instantly, when their necks broke from being hung, but as the child was small, his death was not instant and he was left, suspended and struggling, while everyone else in the camp was forced to witness it. He was still dying when all the other prisoners were made to march past him and look into his face.

A man in the crowd who could take it no more hissed out sarcastically to Wiesel, "Where is God? Where is He?"

Wiesel heard an answer within himself: "Here…hanging on this gallows…"

He could have also said: *and in the Nazis who hung him.* For—"Behold," proclaims God, in *Isaiah* 45:6-7, "both good *and* evil do I create."

God is in *all* beings: the child who is molested; the man who molests him; the policeman who arrests him; the judge who sentences him, and the warden who confines him. God is in everything, making *our moral coming of age* the means by which the Infinite regulates itself.

I had to master myself. And in the last two years of my imprisonment, I was provided with the means to do so.

The Hungry Ghost

I was transferred to work as a clerk-typist at a Southern California prison treatment center for drug addicts. With lush gardens and beautiful trees planted throughout its gently-rolling grounds, the place looked more like a private convalescent center (which it once had been) than a prison, although there was now a chain-link fence around its perimeter, where guard towers holding correctional officers armed with rifles looked down on us to make certain that no one escaped. Instead of cells, we lived in dormitories of one-hundred men each, and as the addicts were only held here for nine months before being released, the atmosphere was a far more relaxed one than would have been found inside a normal penal institution.

Not to say that there wasn't any violence. Five inmates were placed in The Hole one time on suspicion of something-or-another. When investigating officers found that the youngest among them had absolutely nothing to do with whatever the others had been up to, they cut him loose and returned him to the yard. But among narcotics addicts, the only way one man gets released while others continue to be held is through his being a *snitch* and telling on the others, which is considered unforgivable. As a result, on his first day back on the yard, they stabbed him. He was taken away to the hospital, where he later recovered.

You might say it was like the Betty Ford Clinic—with hoodlums.

The men received counseling, took classes in addiction and received specialized training in how to overcome those self-destructive habits that continually led to their undoing. Upon release, they were kept under supervision in the community for several years, but automatically returned for another nine months if they failed to stay clean.

I met a number who had been back, repeatedly. They reminded me of *The Hungry Ghost*—a creature spoken of in Buddhism who is perpetually driven by a thirst he cannot fill, as what he seeks to nourish it with is, like salt water, the very thing that causes his thirst. As I listened to the men describe their cravings, I began to understand that my addiction to sex was no different than theirs. They craved intoxication, just as I did. Like them, what I craved kept me so locked in its embrace that it finally ruled my life as theirs did to them at the expense of everything else—home, job, family, career, and anything else. The conclusion to which this led me was that whatever helped an alcoholic or addict kick his habit might also help me kick mine.

I recalled that book that I had browsed while at an earlier prison, published by Alcoholics Anonymous, that set forth a twelve-step program used successfully by thousands of former compulsive drinkers. Narcotics therapists were now using similar methods and I saw no reason why I could not do so too.

As I watched the men around me come and go (and, so often, return), I listened as they told of their dysfunctional families, whose members actually seemed to have *driven* these men to fail, who seemed to *need* to have them fail so as not to have to face whatever their own deficiencies might have been. It sounded very much like mine, for I had always failed repeatedly too and my parents had always had an excuse ready for me whenever I did, which kept me failing repeatedly.

"Enablers," such people are called in the addiction field, people who are addicted to someone else's always remaining an addict, so they're always needed by him. I've since come to know of a few politicians and community alarmists who are the same way toward us.

It isn't that the addict isn't given *love* by his family. It's that the love given isn't a *healthy* love. It was what Author John Bradshaw calls a *toxic* love, one that poisons its recipient. Instead of helping him to grow, it stunts him.

Like narcotics addicts, alcoholics, and even people who always seem to go from one abusive emotional relationship to another, most sex offenders come from a background where they are unconsciously 'cued' to always injure themselves. Raised in a destructive family setting, many of us—both perpetrators and victims (and how often we both come from the same kind of family!)—soon unconsciously seek to follow paths that lead only to our being abused again and again throughout our lives, cues we have been taught to look for by the families that raised us, among its many suicides, mental cases and emotional dishonesties.

It's a mental conditioning we can only escape by leaving what Best-selling Author Pia Mellody terms *the family trance.*

That was the work that had to be done if any of us were to leave prison and never come back. Very few men in the nation's prisons are ready to do so when they get out and, as a result, most of them keep returning to prisons across the country that are kept in business by not having treatment programs like this one.

Relapse Prevention

At the core of the institution's treatment for addicts was the teaching that, if you simply got honest-enough with yourself to admit that you're tempted by certain situations, you could choose to avoid putting yourself in them. If you drink, for example, every time that you are depressed, whenever you find yourself beginning to feel low, you give yourself *some other way* to deal with it, such as giving yourself some ice cream or a candy bar, or calling someone up from your Alcoholics Anonymous group to help you get past that low.

You don't foolishly tempt yourself, by deliberately putting yourself near the things that your addiction craves, like the person who claims to be a recovering alcoholic but purchases a bottle of whisky *just to have in the house in case guests come over.*

Such a person isn't concerned about guests: he's just trying to see how close he can get to the edge of the wagon before he falls off it.

In the case of a child molester, he might decide to live in a *neighborhood full of children,* or right next door to a school! He might even involve himself in a *youth group.* If he is a rapist, he might take up jogging and run along the same trails that women use. *He might even rent a boat and offer to take some woman out on it!*

To prevent this, one learns to look back and remember the sequence of events that always led up to their offending—in what was called our *offense cycle*—and identify each of those things that always began it: our so-called *triggering mechanisms.*

Were we depressed? Fatigued? Confused? So intoxicated with success that we felt that we could have *anything* now?

What kind of targets tempted us? Young boys, little girls on the edge of adolescence, women who look sad? Only the most ruthless self-honesty works here and the deeper we probe, the stronger we become in avoiding our own destructive urges. Ultimately, we'd know them all, like the FBI knows its Public Enemies, for these are ours.

I had encouragement in doing this inner work. There was a *gun tower* in my yard. Every time I went outside of my dormitory I saw it looking down at me. The message it seemed to be sending was very clear: that if, when I got out, I went back to living the same old way I had lived before I came to prison, it was as certain as tomorrow's sunrise that I would come back to prison and find that same old gun tower looking down on me again.

I could count on it.

I had other encouragement, too. One of the correctional officers under whom I worked decided to invest in me. Every week, on my day off from work, he allowed me to meet with him in his office, where we discussed all the things that might tempt me to relapse once I was released from prison, and how I might sidestep them. We developed what are called *Escape Strategies* I could use, which would allow me to immediately get away from any situation that threatened me with temptation.

Knowing it might not always be possible to get away from some situations immediately, we went further and developed what are called *Coping Strategies,* designed to allow me to handle threatening situations responsibly until I could escape from them.

Week-by-week we went over my record, and as we did so what I finally found was that the thing that caused me to engage in my whole addictive process was *anger* within me for even daring to believe that I could ever succeed in life. It was if some Evil Queen lived deeply within me and demanded to know how I could possibly dare to believe that I was her king.

Again and again, I wilted in her mental presence and engaged in self-destructive habits that 'proved' I wasn't worthy to be anybody's king. I found her origin within my family. Its members were all angry at life and angry at themselves. Rather than take responsibility for having permitted others to abuse them, they lived out their lives as if each of them were the lead singer in a tragic opera, singing for the world's pity and getting only their own.

It was the *family game* and it rapidly became clear that my best interests lay in staying free of it. As one of my counselors warned me about my family, just before I was released from prison: "Look out: you've changed, they haven't."

By the time that Release Day approached, I was holding one of the highest jobs that an inmate could have in prison, working for one of its Acting Wardens as his chief clerk. Out in the yard, I was his spokesperson and in his office I was the men's. Like Joseph, I stood at Pharaoh's right hand. By having chosen that myth at the very beginning, I had activated its power in my own life.

And so it happened that, five years and two months after I had walked in, I left prison and caught a bus and went back to L.A., checking myself in to a quiet, family-run hotel I knew of just at the base of the Hollywood Hills. That evening at sunset I stood at the bottom of the hill that had repeatedly come to me in a vision when my imprisonment had begun and I went up to the temple on top. The Power of my life had kept its promise and I thanked it for having done so.

I had some answers now.

*   *   *

Questions for Group Discussion

1. Can a person convicted of a sex offense return to society and become a member again?

2. Are there some who should not come back, but live in their own colonies, distant from the community?

3. Should our sex offender registration laws also tell you if the sex offender has had any counseling or treatment programs?

4. Should our sex offender registration laws also tell you the method that the offender used to find his victims?

5. What would the sex offender's life look like, if it is described as a journey he is taking?

Chapter Seven

Fate or Free Will

Homecoming

The first morning I was back, my mother came by and took me to brunch. Urging me to name my favorite restaurant, she drove me right over there.

"Have anything you want," she said cheerily, as soon as we were seated.

Relaxing in the embrace of her good will, I ordered my favorite sandwich and exchanged pleasantries with her. I was so relieved that I wasn't going to have to begin my homecoming by having to get into a long, drawn out discussion all about my offense. But the moment my sandwich arrived and I picked it up to take that first delicious bite, she struck:

"*Why* did you do it?"

I was home again.

Setting the sandwich down on my plate, I calmly replied: "The doctors said it was *your* fault."

She snorted at the notion. "Doctors! What do *they* know?"

"Do you still take your high-blood pressure medication?" I asked.

Hurriedly, she opened her purse and peered inside, to make certain she'd brought her capsule of pills. When she looked up again, she saw me smiling at her mischievously and became embarrassed.

Then she struck back. "You can't come to the house, you know. I don't want you up there."

Nervously folding her hands repeatedly, she insisted that it was the fault of other relatives: that they didn't want me up there.

"We'll have lunch again," she assured me, "once each month." Then she quickly reached inside her purse and gave me a folded check with enough money to live on, at least modestly, for my first year back. "Welcome home."

Additional checks would follow if I stayed away.

This was not the time to quarrel with her or force my presence on anyone. It made it lonely for me not to be around my family, especially on holidays, but all things considered it was probably a blessing. At least I wouldn't become one of those taken off parole and sent back to prison because '*the family complained that he made too many problems.*' I knew that I could find other emotional resources, and that's what I concentrated on doing.

Under my state's rules, I would be under the supervision of a parole agent for three years, and I went to report-in to him, as required, the first day of the following week.

I was surprised by how long I was kept waiting in the reception area when I got there, but I figured it was his day to do with me as he wanted, and this was just part of it.

When I was finally shown back to his office, the first thing I noticed was that he was glaring at me from his side of the desk, so I stopped in his doorway rather than come on in.

He said: *"We understand you intend to kidnap your daughter and take her to South America!"*

It didn't take much to figure out who would have concocted a story like that one. Prior to being released on parole, authorities routinely interview a prisoner's family and it was the kind of hysterical claim that only my mother could have made, so I simply nodded and said, "Well, I'll tell you. On Saturday, I had lunch with my mother. At the end of the meal, she gave me this."

Reaching into my shirt pocket, I took out her check and handed it to him. His eyes blinked when he saw the amount it was made out for—more than enough to go to South America—which told him that if I had meant to go there I would have already left.

As he silently passed it back to me I said, "If those allegations were true, I don't really think I'd be here right now, do you?"

He laughed to himself heartily and said, "Well, you know how it is: we hear all kinds of *bull-shit* and just gotta' check it out. Come on in, Goldenflame. I'm sure we're going to have a *very positive relationship.* Congratulations on reporting in on-time!"

We got on fine, from that moment. He had his rules, and I accepted them:

—No drugs

—No drinking

—No contact with my ex-wife or her family

—Not being alone with any child under 14 years of age

—Registering the location of my residence with police,

and

—Seeing an approved psychotherapist during my first year back.

Since I wouldn't be completely free again until I was done with parole, completing it was the only thing that mattered to me. If I'd learned anything from all of the accounts that other men had told me at my last facility, the one thing that made some fail more than any other was their own unwillingness to make success at parole their primary goal.

To avoid that mistake, in addition to the rules that my parole agent gave me, I added four more of my own. I'd recommend them to anybody when they get out of prison:

- **Be off the streets by 10 PM on weekends,** so as not to be around if any trouble breaks out.
- **Avoid any problem area,** for the same reason, and don't do anything to attract the attention of police.
- **When you have an appointment to meet with your parole agent, get there on time and be willing to wait—the rest of the day if necessary, without complaining about it.**
- **Treat your parole agent with respect and you'll be given the same.** Upon his arrival in my room, I always gave him the best chair to sit in, while I sat on the sofa-bed. At the end of each visit, I always

escorted him back out to his car and politely waited until he left before going on my way. In return, he never came over without calling first—and you just can't get it better than that!

Right before I got out of prison, my last counselor had given me the best advice of all as to how to succeed on parole. "Just don't forget," she'd said, "that *you're still in custody.* When you first came in, we kept you behind high walls. During parole, you'll be kept behind *rules.* Treat them as your walls and you'll never have any trouble. Forget that you're in custody and start 'resenting' them and, well, you'll be sent back here again."

I did as she said and it worked.

Where Should a Sex Offender Live?

I wanted a quiet place so there wouldn't be any problems as I'd already heard too many stories about halfway houses where everyone was taken back to prison because of the misconduct of a few. I intended to avoid them.

Jewish facilities were out of the question. Just before my training with the Rabbi ended, he had taken me aside and explained that, because our people were family-oriented, they probably wouldn't want me around, and I accepted that. By looking through a local newspaper I located a rooming house run by a Buddhist organization and I went down there and rented a room that very day. My fellow tenants would be Buddhist *monks* and I wouldn't have enough privacy to tempt me into getting into any improper activities. I also knew that my parole agent would like my being there, as it was a clean, quiet and respectable place, and that was important to me too.

I was right: the first day he came by to see the place, he almost hit his head on the huge bronze gong at the base of the stairs, but he was impressed.

"It's not," he confessed, "what I'm used to seeing when I call on *parolees.*"

Good. That's how I wanted it to stay.

I had to register my address with the police as a convicted sex offender. It was before *Megan's Law*, so I'd been told that my registration would never be made public, but I had my doubts. I felt certain that anyone who wanted to do so could hire a private detective to do a background check and find out if a person was on this list or not. For that same reason, I figured it probably could also be found out by any employer with a good job to offer or a significant promotion later, and I didn't like the limit that seemed to place on me.

I was also uncomfortable with it on a deeper level. A law requiring registration of a whole class of citizens bothered me. It brought back unpleasant memories from my childhood, of muted conversations between relatives in the other room, speaking of Nazi Germany where all of our people had been registered just before being rounded up and shipped off to concentration camps.

That's how it had begun: first the registrations, then the round up and finally the train rides inside box cars to concentration camps for the Final Solution. Could it happen here?

It was in that fearful mood I made my way down to the headquarters of the Los Angeles Police Department to report for registration. I was certain that, at the least, I would probably be facing a bunch of redneck cops gulping coffee out of paper cups as they taunted me for being convicted as a *child molester*.

But, once in the lobby, I was politely informed by a smiling female officer at the information desk that the *registration section* was right down the end of the hall to my right. When I arrived there, instead of Nazi police with spike boots, I found only a mild-mannered young man who was a civilian employee. "Good morning," he said politely, as I entered. "Are you here to register?"

When I replied that I was, he invited me to step over to a desk so that he could fill out a form for me. Moments later, he took my picture and helped me leave my fingerprints on a card, gave me some special jelly and paper towels to clean my hands before leaving and wished me *good luck* as I left.

It'll probably get worse later, I thought, as I left the building. *They're just softening us up.*

The Horoscope of a Sex Offender

I did individual therapy for a year, as ordered by my parole agent. I also enrolled in an adult gym to get back in shape as I'd gained too much weight in prison. And I enrolled in a business school to learn a new occupation that I could practice abroad, after parole ended, for I felt certain that I could never have a future here with a past like mine.

I studied the Hospitality Industry and learned hotel and restaurant management. My schedule became one of classes, gym, homework, Buddhist studies, a weekly visit to the therapist and continued self-studies of my own to learn more about why I'd become what I'd become.

I turned to Greek Tragedy and read the classic drama on incest: Sophocles' play, "Oedipus Rex," about a man doomed at birth by a prophecy that he would grow up to kill his own father and marry his mother. In spite of every step he took to outwit that fate, it came to him anyhow and destroyed his life. The message the playwright gave us was that, whatever the gods foreordain, no man can avoid, and I wondered if that applied to me, so I sent for my astrological horoscope for the first time in my life.

I was *shocked* by what it revealed, for it showed that the reasons for my *entire sexual history* had been written in the stars at the very moment of my birth! The Moon in Scorpio gave me a *compulsive sexuality*, Mars in Scorpio led me to *danger and scandal*, Venus in conjunction with Uranus brought me *unconventional sexual relations with many partners*, Pluto opposite Jupiter gave me *a predatory personality* and Venus in Taurus suggested that I would become *estranged from children*.

I'd been doomed from the very start! What kind of cruel god gave a man a fate like this?

The Ancient Greeks asked that same question and, in Homer's *Iliad*, found their answer. In the character of *Achilles* they had a man who had been given a choice by the gods: between living a long, but anonymous life after which he would be forgotten, or a short but glorious one after which his fame would endure forever.

Obviously, he chose the latter for, upon returning to battle, he brought down Troy's mightiest warrior and, by so doing, made possible the conquest of that kingdom. Before he could see victory, however, he was struck down and killed, but his name is remembered, even today.

Homer's message was clear: we have a choice—*within limits* that are given to us. Astrology said the same thing now to me—when the rest of its findings were included. The sun in Gemini attracts me to *higher thoughts*, my moon in Scorpio also leads me to *work benefiting mankind*, Mars also gives me a strong inner core of *self-reliance*, Uranus in Taurus promises me *freedom through steady growth*, Neptune in Virgo encourages me to *explore the depths* and Neptune trine Uranus offers me *the gift of bringing forth a new vision of unity*, while Pluto in Cancer suggests a life of *marked transformation that could wipe my past clean*.

I'm given challenges, yes, but also opportunities to overcome them. Like Achilles, we are not *doomed* to our fate, but free to determine its outcome by *choosing* among the influences that come to us the ones that *we* will let rule.

The Battle to Tame Lucifer

To keep my sexual urges under control, I never left my premises while they were still gathering strength. Years earlier, I'd been taught some erotic exercises—readily found in many books now—that produce just as much physical satisfaction as a sex act with another person. Anyone can use them and be free afterwards to go back into the world again without being ruled by their sexual urges.

That was certainly better than where I'd been, years before, when I had tried to *suppress* all of my urges until they finally exploded. Fantasies may even be the escape mechanism for urges that would, otherwise, tear society apart. The trick lies in feeding them responsibly, like a pet tiger. If you try to simply starve him, he will ultimately become so desperate that he bursts his cage and devours you.

Not all sex offender therapists would agree, seeing how great a role fantasies play in the lives of some abusers, where fantasies always becomes *plans to be carried out!*

To keep that from happening to me, I always added another ingredient. After each such exercise and fantasy session, I always took a few moments to ask myself what *really* would have happened, had I actually carried out that fantasy?

A number of answers always came to my mind right away: the boy in my fantasy would have told someone else, sooner or later, and I'd have gotten caught. Or: others in the neighborhood would have started noticing that I was bringing kids home, and my parole agent would come out here and take me back to prison. Or, the whole Buddhist facility would become extremely uncomfortable with my living here and expel me.

It would ruin my life again!

And in that moment I could go back into the world again, as I *knew* that it had only been a *fantasy* that I would never seriously plan on carrying-out. I was self-governing now: solidly grounded back in reality, in a world where acts have consequences, and I accepted that.

Psychologists call such a process *aversive conditioning*—coupling an undesirable consequence to any particular act you are contemplating doing. The result is that you stay away from ever committing that kind of act. It works, as I soon found out when my self-control was tested the first time.

I didn't just pay *rent* in the form of money to the Buddhist facility. Like other residents, I also performed some of the chores required to maintain the place. Mine included taking care of the organization's two watchdogs that lived out in the back yard. I fed and watered them each day and made sure that their doghouses were well-secured against winter weather.

When neighboring schoolboys came home each day, I soon noticed that they often stopped by the back fence to say hello to the dogs and, as a result, the boys and I came to know who each other were, at least by sight.

One day, after having a discussion with one of the downstairs residents in my building, I went up to my room to change clothes. A moment later, there was a knock on my door. Thinking it was my fellow resident—come up to continue our conversation—even though I hadn't put my pants back on yet I said, "Come in."

It was one of the boys, a 12-year old, and he had a mischievous look in his eye.

"Hi!" he chirped, as he stepped inside and glanced over at my bed. "Why don't we have a pillow fight?"

A *pillow-fight?*

If my parole agent had walked in at that moment, he would have 'cuffed me and taken me right back to state prison! The rule was clear: *not being alone with any child under 14 years of age!*

Panic began to mount but, at the same time, a wiser voice within urged me not to frighten the child. *It isn't his fault.*

It was time to use a *coping strategy.*

Quickly stepping into some pants, I replied, "That's a *great* idea, but I'll tell you what: the dogs haven't been fed yet. If you'll go downstairs and wait for me in the back yard, I'll be right down and *you* can help me feed them!"

He loved the idea, and skipped right on out...

...as I wiped the *sweat* off my forehead.

He was a nice kid and, afterwards, I walked him up the street to his home, where I asked him to introduce me to his family. When I met his oldest brother, I took the man outside and had a brief talk with him. I said that I thought his younger brother was a very nice little boy, but perhaps needed his brother's help right then.

I told him how the child had shown up in my room, uninvited. "These are times," I said to the older brother, gently, "when it's probably *not* best for a boy of his age to come up to the room of a man of my age, alone. It could spoil the boy's *good reputation.*"

He immediately understood, and promised that he would take care of it.

"Don't scold the boy," I begged. "He did nothing wrong. He just didn't know."

The brother promised to be gentle and I thanked him and left. The problem never occurred again.

But afterwards—in a moment of singular honesty—I couldn't help but wonder if I would remain *just as honest*, once free of the always-possible gaze of my parole agent. Would I really stay as self-controlled, when I was on my own again? Was I really in what the addiction people called *recovery* yet?

I couldn't know, for sure, and for that reason among others, when the time came to choose which country I would go to in order to find a new life when my parole was drawing to its close, I chose one where I believed the consequences wouldn't be as severe as they are here, were I to fail to stay self-controlled there.

I chose Brazil.

Was I just setting myself up for a relapse? By selecting a country where I didn't think that I'd get into that much trouble if I went back to having sex with teenage boys, was I merely *tempting* myself into doing so?

A part of myself really liked the idea of Rio de Janeiro, where there were so many *Street children*.

I decided to get some advice. On the morning that I was to leave for the airport, I asked the *I Ching* what it thought about what I was going to do, and it answered my question with a stinging rebuke, asking me if I had ever considered 'limitations'? That afternoon, when I got on-board the airplane to go to Brazil, I suddenly discovered that I had lost my carry-on bag in the waiting area. It held the only copy I'd packed of the *I Ching*.

Its oracle was no longer speaking to me.

Lucifer chuckled as the plane took off.

*   *   *

Questions for Group Discussion

1. What can families do to help a sex offender complete parole successfully?
2. What can neighbors do?
3. What could you do, if he was living next door to you?
4. What can we ask of neighborhood churches, houses of worship, civics groups, women's groups, men's service organizations, others?
5. What can we ask the media to do?

Chapter Eight

The Myth of Self

Assured of a continuing income from my family if I stayed away, I went abroad and over the next two years tried desperately to find a new life for myself, where I could begin all over again: in four countries on three continents. But, everywhere I went, that *special connection* I needed from life to start a new life remained hidden from me.

I'd hoped that I might find a place where I could *fit right in*—make some friends, find a job, forget my past and go on with my life. But none of those things ripened and, instead, everywhere I went I remained an exile until I realized it was only because I was an exile from myself, no more than an inner nomad.

Adventures in the Amazon Jungle

The day after my parole ended, I flew right into the heart of the Amazon Jungle and landed in Manaus, a northern city in Brazil. My first attempt at making a new start began there. The moment I picked up my luggage at the airport I was approached by a young Brazilian woman wearing the large plastic badge of a tourist guide and I immediately let her know that I didn't want to be solicited. For all my guidebooks had warned me not to sign up for any jungle excursions through such people as less-expensive ones could be found in town.

"Besides," I told her, my mind still on that carry-on luggage I'd lost, "the first thing I have to do right now is buy some more anti-malaria medication." For that, too, had been in the bag.

"Oh!" she eagerly volunteered. "I can help you! There are only two *far-macias* in town that sell it, and I know where one is. I can drive you there!"

It seemed strange to me that, in the middle of the Amazon Jungle, there'd only be *two* places where anti-malarial medication would be sold, but I decided I'd better take her offer as I didn't know where either of them were located.

"Okay," I said. "But I don't want to buy any excursions."

She nodded understandingly and escorted me toward the doors of the terminal. The moment we stepped outside, the jungle's scorching air hit me like a blast furnace.

"*Quente!*" I said: the Portuguese word for "hot."

"*Sim*," she replied: the Portuguese word for "yes." I'd spent my last six months taking an audio course in that language and it was a pleasure to begin using it.

It didn't take long to reach downtown Manaus, a modern-looking metropolis hacked right out of a jungle that waits patiently behind it—like a crouching cheetah—to pounce on it and take it back at any time.

True to her word, my companion delivered me to a pharmacy where they sold what I was looking for, then asked if I would walk *just a couple of doors down the street* to meet her boss, "so he won't feel I wasted my time today."

How *convenient* that his office was so close. But I owed her for her help, and the ride into the city, so I went with her just to meet the man.

His name was Armando and from his first words I could tell that he was in love with the Amazon Jungle. Lean, tall, dark-haired, his words held me spellbound as he told of all the wonders that the jungle offered. I was so impressed by his delivery that I signed up for an excursion due to leave in just three days. In return, he had the young woman get on the phone and book me a hotel room that wound up costing me only half of what I'd been prepared to pay. They even gave me a ride on over there.

It was a fine little place, only a fifteen-minute walk from the Amazon River. Anxious to see that magnificence, I quickly unpacked my luggage and made my way on down there.

The Amazon River is a breathtaking sight, so indescribably vast as it flows past. The city's largest marketplace sits high above its banks. Underneath a long, shady roof, row after row of every kind of meat, fish, vegetable and fruit grown or caught anywhere in the region sits on display, for everything in the Amazon is brought here by riverboat or carried away.

The river is the jungle's major artery, feeding it from Peru in the west to the Atlantic Ocean 2500 miles to the east. Every night at sunset, people go down to the river and drink a toast to her, using a local beer kept just-above freezing. It's called *cerveza gelado*, which means 'frozen beer,' and in-between its rich cold temperature and high alcoholic boost, it's like an ice pack made to smother the heat inside you.

"*Ele vai a Peru*," the people sing out, as they raise their bottles in salute to the setting sun, knowing it's rising elsewhere now. "*He goes to Peru!*"

I bought a beer and sat on top of a low wall to enjoy the view. The heat had drenched the back of my thin cotton shirt and the beer flowed sweetly into me as I sat there and looked at the scene before me: the boats, the men, the River…the Power of my life!

An old man glanced at me as he walked past and I politely raised my beer in salute. In response, he taught me my first Amazon wisdom: "If you keep looking at the river long-enough," he said, "you will see all your old enemies go floating on by!"

Several days later, I went into the jungle through one of the river's fingers on the city's edge. Armando had guides take us in by canoe and the moment we reached our lodge I asked him if I could leave it to step into the bush.

He smiled knowingly, for he understood the spell that called. "Just don't go too far," he said. "And, if you see any animals, don't forget that this is not a zoo! Here, they will eat *you*."

I promised to take care and hiked on over to our compound's border. Gently pushing my way through some of the waiting shrubbery, I stepped into the jungle and found myself in an entirely pristine and primitive world: of plants and jousting treetops whose branches all pushed and shoved at each other in their struggle to get to the life-giving sunlight high above.

Not far ahead, I saw a tree at least sixty or seventy-feet tall and went over to sit under it just to let myself meditate in the jungle's steamy cleanliness. A small rivulet of the Amazon flowed silently past. The stillness all about me was so great that I could almost touch it.

At first. But then, high above in the canopy, I suddenly heard the crackling noises of dry leaves being rudely kicked off as a small troop of tree monkeys scampered across. Tan, dusty leaves swirled lazily on down in their wake, falling to the ground nearby, where waiting platoons of army ants quickly chopped them up and marched them back to their nest. In the jungle, everything comes back to the soil, which is both grave and womb of life.

A vision appeared in my mind, of a giant sitting in front of me, insanely devouring his own foot——while a new one grew out from behind him.

I took heart from the message I saw in this: that life is self-renewing only through being self-destructive. It *can't* recreate itself without first destroying itself; like a snake that sheds its skin so that a new one can come forth. Self-destruction leads to self-renewal. Our lives are *built* to fail—repeatedly—so that they may succeed over and over again. I still had a chance!

I spent almost a week there, hiking through the bush and gazing with wonder at huge rubber trees and brightly-colored parrots. I was taken to a small waterfall where I let myself have a natural shower underneath it. Afterwards, while making my way along the trail back to camp, I came across a gigantic spider web almost two yards wide. All along its many strands I could see dozens of tiny insects stuck to it, quivering for their lives. I paused to watch as Mother Death came creeping down to have her late afternoon meal.

Armando saw my look of pity and said, "Do not waste your sympathies on them. They are *Anopheles.*"

The mosquitoes that carry malaria?

"*Bon appetit!*" I called to the spider, and walked past her uncaringly. May she eat all of them.

Meeting My Adversary

A few days later, I was back in the city, only to find that I had contracted Jungle Fever. I woke up with it in my hotel room at dawn, hot and very ill. When I rummaged through my luggage enough to use my thermometer, I could barely believe what it told me: I had a temperature of 102 degrees Fahrenheit. Quickly, I took two aspirins and lay down, falling asleep for a couple of hours. When I woke back up, I took my temperature again.

It was 105.

It should be *down!*

The aspirins weren't having any effect and I knew that I was in danger. If I didn't get some medication right away, brain damage would occur and then death.

I forced myself to get dressed and stumbled out of the hotel into a waiting taxi, which I had take me down to Armando's, as he was the only person I knew.

The moment I appeared in his doorway, he got up from his desk.

"You look terrible!" he said.

I told him what was happening and he came over, felt my forehead and gestured toward the door. "We'll go to the *farmacia.*"

He bought me something from West Germany: forty drops poured into a glass of juice and my fever immediately began to cascade down. By the next morning it was normal. Armando came by and urged me to *convalesce.* "You're still getting used to our climate and its biota," he said. "It's totally different than the one you have in North America, with many germs your body hasn't experienced before. Rest some more"

I thanked him, then asked a question I had been wondering about since arriving in Manaus. "How come there are only two *farmacias* that sell anti-malaria medication?"

He laughed gently to himself before replying, "Because they don't need it here. They conquered malaria in this city many years ago. Only *tourists* buy it now."

I did as he said and took it easy for the next week or so, staying close to my hotel. When the day came that I felt well-enough to do so, I went back on down to the Amazon River, thinking I might have a cold beer there and perhaps something simple to eat.

The moment I stepped through the ornate gate to its market place, however, I was besieged by a whole swarm of local shoeshine boys, ten or eleven years old, all of whom began petitioning for my business at-once. In response, I brushed them away like mosquitoes. But then, from out of the shadows, another boy stepped forward, smiling wickedly. He looked to be about fourteen or fifteen years old and moved his lithe little hips like a Latin dance as he approached.

I was immediately frozen to the spot.

All over the world there are boys like him, wise beyond their years in the ways of the street. Sexually-used since who-knows-when, they know that an older man, traveling alone, is a likely customer and they move like a spider in the jungle toward their own *Anopheles*.

The gleam in his eyes transfixed me and I could feel my self-control getting ready to melt away. Within seconds, I would just be an urge again.

Suddenly, my bright new life flashed in front of me—the adventures I was having in the jungle, my friendship with Armando, the welcoming staff at my hotel, a deferential police officer, up at the plaza, who always tipped his cap to me as I strolled past—all this would vanish if I lost control.

The boy would boast to his friends, who would tell their older brothers, who would beat and rob me while police looked the other way, if they didn't shake me down for money themselves. Instead of being a welcome guest, I would become everyone's prey.

I was at that *threshold magnitude* of evil of which Solzhenitsyn had written. Had I gone so far past it that I couldn't make my way back now?

The boy continued to dance toward me and I knew there were only seconds left before I went off with him, compulsively.

Looking deeply within myself for some way out, I plunged my right hand into my pants pocket and pulled out a fist full of coins that I hurled over his head. He immediately turned to look as all the other boys hungrily followed their arc through the air, and then rushed to join them as everyone chased after them...leaving me *free* to turn around and walk quietly back to my own neighborhood, still whole.

I was no longer just an urge. I had attained *personhood*.

The Dance of Life

I found a book in Portuguese and began translating a part of it each day into English, to improve my language skills. At night, I took a break from my studies by wandering up the street to the nearby outdoor cantina, where I bought a bottle of ice cold beer to beat back the jungle heat that lingered on, even after sunset.

Rarely was I left alone very long for, in addition to the some of the locals who were naturally curious about people from other countries, the streets were flooded each night with hordes of little boys, Ages 10 and under, all with trays hung around their necks, upon which sat tiny packets of chewing gum or small bags of peanuts they had shelled and rolled themselves to sell to anyone they could find. While all of these children needed charity, none of them sought it. Poor, they certainly deserved it. But the Brazilians are a proud people and do not ask for anything without offering something in return.

As I knew that it would be impossible to buy from all of these boys since there were so many of them, I quickly began doing as the locals did, avoiding eye-contact with any as they approached my table while I waved the forefinger of my left hand back and forth in the air a couple of times in a signal they understood to mean *please leave me alone*, which they respected.

They always did, until one night when one little boy walked up to me and refused to go away.

Curious, I finally looked up and what I saw was the pain in his eyes. He was ten years old, with blond hair and brown eyes and just right then it was obvious that, if he didn't get a victory, his little soul would shatter.

I nodded with a knowing smile and took out some coins from my pocket as I recalled how all the guidebooks had urged me to always be generous here. You pay more for your airline ticket, they cautioned, than most of these people earn in a year. As a result, they think you are a millionaire and expect you to share some of what you have. It's only good manners to do so.

That's when I decided to buy from this child, regularly, as my *representative* of all the rest. I told him that he could sell to me from now on, whenever he saw me.

He smiled gratefully and went away. But, as he did so, I confessed to myself that I also found him potentially attractive. *In just a few years...*

That's how the Lucifer Complex works. While those of us subject to it may wish to believe we are as normal as anyone else, the truth is that we are not. We have a *myth* of self as to who we think we are. But, like the alcoholic, whenever we are near our temptation that myth begins to vanish as all sense of being separate from the temptation begins to dissolve. If we don't take immediate steps to prevent it, we will become the temptation and then feed it.

We aren't *lying* when we tell you that we don't mean to harm the child/rape the woman: we're lying to ourselves because we haven't accepted the fact that such an impulse will always be within us. If we get too close to our prey, it runs right through us, and we strike before even we know it. The answer, as I was finding, is to stay away from even getting near our prey.

A few evenings later, it was an especially hot night—with a humidity that was smothering—when I saw the boy next. Because of the unusual heat, I asked him if he would like a cold soda drink and he smiled his assent. I signaled to a passing waiter-to give him a cold soft drink, on my bill—and the boy thanked me sincerely. But when the bottle arrived and he was about to raise it, he suddenly halted midway and looked about.

Spying two little cousins across the street, he signaled for them to come over and then—*in spite of the fact that this was his only drink*—he let each of them drink first. His unselfishness was so great that it shamed me into finding my own and I immediately dropped nourishing any further thought of using him as a sexual target. I respected him, instead, subsequently learning that he had several brothers and sisters with whom he lived, along with his mother. I never heard anything about his father and knew better than to ask. In the mornings, he went to school; in the afternoons, he shined shoes, and in the evenings carried a tray around his neck and sold gum or small sacks of peanuts to contribute what he could to the household income.

He said that he wanted to become an airline pilot when he grew up and fly huge airplanes that crossed whole continents. I told him that, if he wanted to enough, *he could even have the stars!*

My recovery was solidifying and I never got to Rio de Janeiro to go after any of its street children.

It wasn't much later that I learned the Portuguese word for the *intimate* form of the pronoun "you"—-used between *lovers*—-is the very same word I had used years before to first name my sexual compulsion before I was told that others call it *Lucifer*: *voce*. Yet I'd never spoken or known Portuguese before this time. How could I have used it so accurately years ago unless our compulsion *is* our lover—a deadly lover—who draws us closer and closer until we're extinguished within its embrace? Apparently, consciousness was trying to tell me the same thing it had whispered to the Sufi poet, Rumi, eight centuries before: *our creator and we do not finally meet somewhere, but are in each other all along.* What's necessary is that we learn to respect the fact that it has a dark side, too: "both good *and* evil do I create." It has to be this way, so that *all* of its children may eat.

Encoded within everyone's life is the life of an Other. Finding that Other and learning to dance with it is the game of life. Sometimes it leads, and sometimes we do. The 'trick' is to notice whose turn it is, as soon as possible, every time the dance changes.

The Polite Interrogation

When my visa expired, I went north—to Costa Rica—and that's when I began writing this book. While on parole I had made one new friend and told him that I'd just gotten out of prison, but not why. He was decent-enough not to ask. But he did say that if I ever chose to write my story and send it to him—if it was commercial-enough—he could send it to an agent he knew and have it published. Having no other options, I decided to start it now.

I rented a room with a kitchen, outside the capital city, bought a used electric typewriter and worked on the book six days a week, taking Fridays off to do banking and any errands that were necessary. I always included a nice meal at a restaurant at the end of that day. One time, reading an English-language newspaper over coffee, I spotted a notice announcing services for Americans overseas at a local Jewish temple. Homesick by now,

I went over there and enjoyed the experience so much that I began return-ing regularly. But in the social hour afterwards, I found myself so on-guard against saying anything about my past that I was unable to make any but the most distant of new acquaintances.

Only in the movies does one effortlessly slip away to a foreign country and begin a new life. In the real world, one's past sticks to them and when it's not a nice past there are always the awkward questions; the social inquiries one faces whenever one meets new people abroad.

"What did you do in the States?"

"Are you married?"

"Do you have any children?"

Additional questions always follow until the other person has sorted and filed you into a known category. *Oh, a retired businessman. I see. A lawyer? How nice.*

What was I going to tell them: that I was a *retired sex offender?*

Of course, in answering, one could always lie about one's past (and any-one escaping their past always wants to do that). But if you do, you'll quickly realize that the burden of having to remember all the lies you told soon becomes too great for anyone without a laptop computer. ("Oh—I said that I have *three* children? Well, actually that's true, but my second wife also had two of her own from an earlier marriage and *that's* why I often say that I have five…worked there instead of here…lived in that city instead of this one…")

One who really wishes to be rid of one's past doesn't actually get rid of it; one learns instead how to 'minimize' it by saying no more than is absolutely essential to social discourse and then changing the subject.

That works, and as a result one passes the moment of inquisition. But, afterwards, there is always that sense of *distance* still out there—which leaves you as uncomfortable as it does relieved that you didn't have to dis-cuss what you wished would just go away. And because it's always possible that someone from your past might just show up—on *their* vacation—you always keep your suitcase open in case you have to pack hurriedly.

Of course, you can always avoid your fellow countrymen and just socialize with locals, if you know the language (or they know yours, which is more often the case). That works, as the *language barrier* exempts you from having to go into the details of your past. No one expects you to know the local language so well that you could refer to all the details of anything, including your past. Thus, one can always use the foreign language to say "I don't understand your question" when asked something you'd really prefer not to have to answer, and get away with it.

But you still know who you are; you don't forget that, or the life you've lived up until then. You're reminded of it all the time, wherever you go. You're on a bus going into town and see a woman walking along the pavement with two little boys, one holding on to each of her hands. Instantly, you flash back to your own wife of years ago, and your sons when they were with her and—what do you know?—emotionally, you're right back home again, in your own country and not anywhere near the Third World refuge you thought you'd found.

Key holidays such as Christmas and New Year's, of course, destroy any possibility of forgetting one's past and they occur everywhere. So, no, that quaint romantic notion that one can easily fly into a foreign country and effortlessly become someone else is just the cheap fiction of paperback novels and made-for-television movies. One never leaves their past, for it is as much a part of them as their skin. All one can do is wear a coat over it and squirm inside every time you meet anyone from your own country and they begin to pursue that *polite interrogation.*

When my visa here expired, I moved again, to Mexico to finish writing the manuscript for this book. Just before I left Costa Rica, I sent a letter to my friend in L.A. and told him all about my past.

No Future After All

When the time later came that I felt the manuscript was ready to be seen, I flew up to L.A. and hand-delivered it to him.

He refused to accept it because of what he had learned from my letter. "I could have forgiven you for what you were sent to prison for," he said, hurt and angry. "But not for your having kept it from me for so long, as if you didn't trust me. Our friendship is at an end. I don't ever want to see you again."

I left his company, feeling crushed, even though it was my own fault and I knew it. Totally without hope, when I walked past a trashcan in back of a supermarket in Hollywood, I dumped the manuscript inside it and went on my way. Still shunned by my family, I stayed at a hotel and by the time a week had gone past I was so despondent that I began considering going back to living as a sexual predator again, as nothing else seemed to offer any reason not to do so. The same old process had kicked-in once more: whenever I became too depressed, like any other sex offender, lust came up as its antidote. You might want to consider that, the next time someone suggests that the best way to handle registered sex offenders is simply by driving them away.

I went to a bookstore and bought myself some travel books to find a destination. In reading about various places in Central America, I came across an orphanage that allowed anyone to live there while serving as a volunteer.

Kids! Living with them.

My mind caught fire at the very thought of it.

Yes. That's where I'll go. The hell with this! Being a sex offender is all I've got. That's who I really am.

The Third World is full of European and American child molesters, working in settlement projects, orphanages and any other place where they can nurse their sexual addiction until they die, or go mad, or get killed. I felt ready to become one of them and take my place in the armies of the lonely.

I made my way down to Mexico City that week, in the first leg of my new journey. But the further I got from the toxic atmosphere of rejection I'd just left behind me, the less the whole purpose of the trip seemed to appeal to me and, by the time I reached Mexico City, I was absolutely repulsed by the notion. Freed from everything that had depressed me, my wholeness had returned.

But where was I to go now?

A local Jewish family provided the answer. They invited me to join them for a Sabbath dinner in their home and, when I got there, I found myself surrounded by all their many relatives, a number of whom had been to Israel several times. When the oldest uncle present leaned over his soup bowl to ask me if I had ever gone there, all I could say was, "Not yet."

He looked back at me, leaving a tablespoon suspended in mid-air. "What are you waiting for? *That's the only place where a Jew can find a new life!*"

I flew there the very next day, certain that this time my past would not come along.

Ambushed by My Past

Upon arrival at the Tel Aviv Airport, a hand gently clasped my shoulder as I spoke to the operator on a pay phone to let my family's attorney know where I was now.

I turned my head to see who was touching me and beheld a young man with a crew cut who spoke with an accent. "Israeli Security," he said." You've got to leave the airport."

I immediately wondered to myself: *'Because I'm a convicted sex offender? They know?'*

As I looked around, I saw others like him hustling hordes of fellow tourists outside.

No! I suddenly realized. *It's because there's a Bomb Threat!*

I quickly turned and followed the crowd into the street.

A woman in her early forties stood in the roadway outside of the airport, a Westerner clutching her baggage cart. She was frozen into place by terror and I comforted her. "There's nothing to fear," I told her as I approached. "We're safe." I could feel it.

She blinked and came back to where we were. "What should we do?"

I looked up the street and said, "Why don't we join the others?"

She pushed her baggage cart ahead of her as the two of us walked up to do so. Thanks to what she told me later, when the emergency was past and we had a cup of coffee together inside of the airport, I learned of a great place to stay in nearby Jerusalem and hailed a cab to make my way on over.

I landed in the Arab Quarter and happily booked a room with a view of the entire city from my building's rooftop. Once unpacked, I headed back out into the streets and began to tramp my way into ancient history with each step, for many of the stones upon which I walked had been placed there by any number of conquerors who had walked here before: Egyptians, Romans, Turks, Crusaders, Germans and later the British.

Even Christ.

I bought a ticket and climbed on top of the city's walls and walked around them, seeing two kinds of history at the same time, the ancient city inside and the modern one, outside.

I visited the Church of the Holy Sepulcher, where Christ was said to have been crucified. I meandered through a humble Ethiopian monastery. And I edged my way through a long stone tunnel that finally emerged into an open stone courtyard as large as several city blocks, where the Western Wall of King Solomon's Temple now stands majestically in the distance. Every Friday night, the city's most religious Jews pray there.

I was charmed by Jerusalem but it was an expensive charm. In spite of its Third World location, its prices were more like those of Beverly Hills and I soon found that my funds would not sustain me unless I lived in more modest quarters. A move to a much simpler place, where the owner gave me a discount on my room in exchange for manning the front desk at night, provided the remedy.

On my first Friday night off from work there, I made my way back to the Wall of King Solomon's Temple and left my late father's name written down on a slip of paper in-between two large stones in the wall, as is the custom there. After I did so, I pressed the side of my face against the wall and closed my eyes.

All around me, others prayed in Hebrew.

A moment passed, then two. And out of the very center of my consciousness, I suddenly heard my own voice inside my head, proclaiming in a very-loud whisper: *"I AM!"*

Startled, I stepped back from the Wall and acknowledged the *power* it held with a nod of my head and then went back to my hotel.

Perhaps some of the wall's power was still with me when I got there, for that night one of our guests—a college coed from London—came down to talk with me, as many of the other students did on other nights. They'd speak of their hopes and their fears and their plans for the future. My visitor tonight spoke of her memories, and as she was telling me of her child-hood—all of a sudden—her eyes began to brim and her voice cracked.

"Oh, Jake!" she cried. "How am I ever going to love my father again? He *molested* me when I was only five years old!"

It was as if my past was suddenly standing there, pointing its long accu-satory finger right at me. My run was over and I knew it. No matter where I went, it would always be waiting to ambush me again. There would always be another moment like this, when it would unexpectedly appear, always be some other person to ask me that same kind of question. It was time to face that fact and accept my past instead of trying to hide it, like one's wedding ring in front of an attractive woman I've just met.

I flew back to the United States the following week determined to use my past as the foundation for the only decent life I saw that I could have now: working with other men who have a similar past.

My myth of self was a more honest one now.

*   *   *

Questions for Group Discussion

1. What are some of the things that might cause a recovering sex offender to just 'give up'?
2. What is the most likely outcome if he is just rejected and driven away?
3. Do you believe that our lives are designed to succeed over the failures in its past? Can a former sex offender build a new life?
4. What are some of the most wholesome things that the community can do to encourage sex offenders to regain self-control?
5. Could you bring yourself to tell someone else that *you* once committed a sexual offense, if that were true?

Chapter Nine

Sex Offender in the Community

It was not a good time to be a convicted sex offender in the world. From Australia to the United Kingdom and throughout the United States, there had been a stream of ugly incidents against us. Pickets had appeared, demanding we move, realtors were afraid to sell our houses, and in England a 14-year old girl died after the building in which she had been staying was burned down after having been mistakenly identified as one harboring some of us. Cries went up, demanding that we all be rounded up and expelled, either to a special town of our own or to an island from which we'd never be allowed to leave.

In the previous regime in South Africa, a similar policy banning all Black people from living in the cities was called *apartheid*. What I was looking at now was *sexual apartheid*.

How strange. Almost all of us had originally been victims of sexual abuse and, in Western society, when you're a victim of sexual abuse, people fall all over themselves feeling sorry for you. But the moment it turns out that the damage we received passes through us to go on and damage someone else, all of a sudden we're no longer victims.

"They're like *Dracula*!" declared one judge, in a case I'd worked.

If he'd meant the kind described by Novelist Anne Rice, he'd have been right, for vampires in her novels don't choose to become vampires, they're made into them by someone who already is one. Similarly, among all the sex offenders I've met—in the jails, or through the mails or on the Internet or in the streets—there's never been one yet who was able to tell me that he *chose* to become a sex offender. We don't *choose* our sexual inclination any more than you do.

Confirmation can be found in the work of one of America's top therapists for sex offenders, Dr. Fred Berlin, of Johns Hopkins University
School of Medicine, in Baltimore, Md., whose sex offender treatment
clinic has the lowest re-offense rate in this nation. According to his findings, no one chooses their sexual tastes:

"The author, for example, is a man who is attracted exclusively to
females rather than males. Although he might find a broad age range of
females to be appealing in a sexual way, he is not attracted to 4-year-old
females, nor is he attracted sexually to 80-year-old females. Thus he does
not refrain from having sex with young children only because he is a moral
person. He is simply not tempted sexually by young children…

"If one looks at a group of children who have been active sexually with
adults, thankfully most do not grow up to…(become child molesters).
However, (modern day sex offender therapist pioneer A.N.) Groth and
others have shown that if one looks at a group of men who (are child
molesters)…the overwhelming majority were active sexually with adults
during childhood. Thus, if one wishes to use words such as victim and victimizer, it appears that many men with pedophilic sexual orientations are
in fact simply the former victims of sexual abuse during childhood, grown
up…sexual orientation is much like language…Once (it)…has been
acquired (it)…cannot simply be made to go away."

As Dr. Berlin concludes:

"Thus it seems difficult to see how a person could be considered blameworthy because he is sexually attracted to children. However, it could be
argued that although it is not his *fault* that he is sexually attracted to children, it is still his *responsibility* to resist succumbing to such temptations."

Levels of Recovery

Upon returning from Jerusalem, I landed in Los Angeles and even then I
was tested again. While on a walk by myself the next afternoon, I saw three
boys in their late teens across the street. Two of them seemed to be trying
to urge the third to do something, while glancing at me repeatedly. My
danger signals came on immediately. And a moment later, the third boy

turned my way and began coming over to my side of the street: a blond-haired kid, about seventeen I'd guess.

He was carrying himself rather awkwardly and when he came up to me I could see that he had beads of perspiration on his upper lip, which told me he was scared.

He asked me with a bit of hesitation if he could have some money and I knew it was his first time. That I could easily take him back to my room and get away with using him was clear: no one else was around who knew me, I'd be flying out the next day and these kids would never find me. And he wasn't a bad-looking boy, certainly attractive-enough to consider.

But when I looked inside of myself, I found a *firewall* present that had never been there before, and it wouldn't give way. My recovery had strengthened.

"No," I replied firmly, and the boy turned around and walked back to his friends somewhat sheepishly as they stood there, not quite knowing what to do. I could resume living safely in my country now, although I would always have to remain on-guard.

Recovery doesn't happen on just one level. It goes on and becomes recovery on many levels. First, it may be no more than a fear of getting arrested again and sent back to prison, so you don't re-offend. Then, it may be a matter of not wanting to lose whatever self-esteem you've been able to find. Later, it becomes a concern for those you might otherwise victimize. Ultimately, it goes on to become concern for their families as well as for those who have trusted you to remain self-governing. Recovery never ends. It just keeps deepening until you don't want to do anything more than honor your new life by taking care of it.

That doesn't mean you won't be tempted to re-offend at times. Like every human being, as long as your heart beats you will have urges that come to you. Most of the time they will be quickly passing ones, of no concern. Occasionally, they may be threatening and that is when all your training will pay off. I told Oprah that no one can say *for certain* that they won't re-offend, because sex offending isn't curable. That means there will always be a chance of relapse for any of us, no matter how small. As a result, when she found that I had given a former victim my vow never to re-offend, that troubled her as it seemed to conflict with what I'd already said.

The fault is mine: I didn't express myself clearly-enough. While it's true there will always be a chance of relapse—making it impossible to say with *absolute certainty* that I won't re-offend—by giving someone my vow, what I'm telling them is that it is still my *intention* never to do so. And that's what makes it worth giving. But the question she was pursuing is an essential one: can we ever trust sex offenders again?

The answer is as old as the story of the scorpion that hopped on a frog's back and asked for a ride across the river, then stung the frog halfway across. "Why did you do that?" the frog asked him, in agony, "Now we're *both* going to drown!"

"Because," said the scorpion. "I'm a scorpion!"

What that tells us is that the wise person will never ask a convicted sex offender to do certain things: like, baby sit their child. But, wash their car? Why not?

I would never take a job as a boy's high school swim coach. That would be accepting an invitation to a likely disaster. But that doesn't mean I can't serve you in other ways. It doesn't mean that those convicted of sex offenses can't find work where they won't be threatening anyone. Obviously, if they are not given any kind of work, they will join the armies of the desperate, far too large already out on our streets. One man I know of, who was convicted of being a Sexually Violent Predator and has now been released from mental hospital confinement, is currently seeking work that he can do on his computer from out of his home. That could be an excellent job for him, and no reason for anyone else not to use him, so long as his work is honest.

We cannot afford to have an underclass in our society. We're at war now, and the war may return to our shores once again. A divided society is not something we can afford. What keeps a society great is its ability to heal, and that means heal its people: even those injured by mental conditions they never chose. Twenty-one hundred years ago, a great man died on a cross to teach resurrection. We crucify him again every time we deny it to anyone else.

The Scarlet Letter

My recovery began to flourish when I settled in San Francisco. I found a room in the center of town, rode the Cable Car into Chinatown and took a bus across the Golden Gate Bridge to go hiking in a nearby redwood forest. I began attending worship services at an ecumenical inner city church, where its legendary pastor welcomed me after I had confided in him and told him of my past.

Not certain that others would be as charitable, I decided to behave only as a guest in the community and not as one of its equals. *Toleration* is what I'd seek for now and let acceptance wait until later. In my relationships with others, I began living by a new rule: *no dishonest friendships.* Having already lost one good friend out of waiting too long to tell him about my past, I decided that I'd rather not have any if the only kind I could have were based on concealment. So I kept my watch and whenever I saw anyone approaching that line transforming an acquaintance into a friend, I'd tell them about my past, with an apology, and let them know that I didn't intend to repeat it.

They appreciated such a disclosure, and let me have a place among them. As word about me got around, women who had been sexually abused began seeking me out: just to listen respectfully, as they narrated an account of their own suffering. Afterwards, each time, I always apologized to them—as if I had been their abuser—for I knew that I could have been, and they accepted that. As a result, both of us went away from such encounters feeling a bit more healed.

And so it happened that, when the law was changed to require not only the *registration* of sex offenders but *dissemination of their residential locations* to the public—under Megan's Law—it was easy for me to endorse it and I did so, speaking in the press and on television from the time it came into force. This new law was doing no more than insisting upon what I had already found just made good sense: that the most effective way to prevent a sex offender from repeating his crime is by making him known to all those around him so that they may become his guardians.

As far as I could see, it was a good law, for it protected the public from sex offenders, by letting the public know who we are, while protecting us from ourselves, by reminding us of who we have been—every time we go into a police station to register—so that we don't become that kind of person again.

It doesn't send police out to our homes to round us up and take us in to register, but leaves the responsibility to do so on us, as it should in a democracy. And that makes it the most gentle deterrent that anyone could design.

Those who want to claim that, by its permanent display of our criminal records, *Megan's Law* compels us to wear a *Scarlet Letter* would be best advised to read Nathaniel Hawthorne's classic novel of that same name. Like us, his main character—Hester Prynne—was found guilty of a sex crime: adultery, and made to let the community know of it for the rest of her life by being forced to wear a large letter "A" of scarlet material on her dress.

Undoubtedly, everyone expected her to flee rather than bear such a punishment. But, to their surprise, Hester not only wore the letter and remained there, she also accepted her punishment as a call to walk a path of penance and did so, being of service to anyone suffering from misfortune. In time, women particularly turned to her for counsel and, well before the end of her days, Hester Prynne succeeded in taking what had been meant as a 'badge of shame' and transforming it into becoming a badge of service that brought her respect from all.

Not a bad idea. And perhaps that's why a sex offender registration and notification lawn now exists—in one form of another—not only in the United States, but under eight other governments as of this writing:

Australia
Canada
Ireland
Republic of Korea, and
United Kingdom of England, Wales, Northern Ireland and Scotland.

In two of those countries—Australia and Ireland—anyone who is already a registered sex offender in their home country must also register there when arriving as a tourist, if they plan to remain beyond a certain number of days, and other countries may follow suit. Sex Offender Registration Laws are in the world to stay, whether they come to be called Megan's Law (U.S.), Christopher's Law (Canada), Sarah's Law (United Kingdom) or any other.

Taking Vows

I met a Zen Buddhist priest, and he invited me to join a local meditation group. Several months later, its members invited me to take the same first vows given to every monk in that religion (*jukai*) and I did so. Then one more was added: because of my background, several of the senior members asked that I dedicate myself to helping anyone injured by sexual abuse. "That'll be your 'beat,'" they said. "We'll take care of the others." And that's been my practice since.

The ceremony took place in a northern California redwood forest, where we had gone to meditate for a week. Upon my return to San Francisco, one of the news organizations informed me that, at the same time I'd been taking vows, another sex offender in that same area had also gone into the forest and hung himself, apparently in shame after police had distributed his photo in the nearby community.

What an unnecessary loss. Americans are the most forgiving people in the world—if you trust them first. But if you don't, and they find out about you on their own, they cannot be blamed if they also wonder what else you may be hiding about yourself.

If the man had only told his neighbors about his past, the poster would not have troubled him and that is why I tell all those who find it hard to be registered: *If you want to overcome Megan's Law, become Megan's Law and tell people yourself about your past.*

Practicing My Vows

I started a prison outreach project, writing to convicted sex offenders in penitentiaries all over the country, urging them to seek counseling and study themselves, so they can start their recovery before they get back out.

I began a Web site for my fellow sex offenders (www.calsexoffenders.net), explaining Megan's Law in laymen's terms and listing its various requirements. Writing openly as one of them, I encouraged them to obey the registration law and remain self-controlled. Originally limited only to providing the details of that law, it was later expanded to include a list of recovery resources, worldwide, for anyone seeking help in dealing with sexual compulsions.

Subsequently, I included a crisis counseling page for those who had lost control, committed the very worst of crimes, and now were in hiding as fugitives. Having been close to that myself at one point, I sought to call these men back by telling them how they could contact legal help and arrange their safe surrender to police so that they could continue to have a life they could restore.

It worked better than I would have thought. When a wave of child kidnappings and murders broke out across the country, one man used the site's e-mail link to confess he had similar urges and ask for counseling. With the aid of several national referral services that I was able to contact, and the help of several local therapists who guided me, the man was given two qualified clinicians to help him within twenty-four hours and he later wrote to say that he had entered a counseling program. Who knows how many children that saved? The man is a hero, for he bested himself.

The following year, I was invited to an international conference in the United Kingdom where I was allowed to facilitate dialogue groups for former victims of abuse, standing openly among them as a former abuser.

Every convicted sex offender can make a similar effort if he or she is willing to do so.

Cutting Through the Mountain

I wanted to find my now-adult daughter and at least offer her an apology. But no one in my family knew where she lived. Right after I went to prison, her family broke off all contact with mine and no one ever heard from them again. When I got back, and had a lawyer tell my ex-wife's attorney that I was willing to resume child support payments, my offer was declined, leaving me without any way of knowing where they might be now.

Several years later, while in town between trips abroad, I ran into a mutual friend who told me that he had seen my ex-wife. "She invited me over to see your daughter."

"Really?" I exclaimed. But, before I could ask further, he said that the visit had been cancelled at the last minute. "She said they were still living with your ex-wife's mother, who refuses to let your daughter meet *anyone* who has ever known you."

That was then. Now, my daughter was an adult and could be living anywhere, making the only way of finding her one of having an attorney hire a private investigator to locate her.

Before taking such a step, I decided to put the idea before several women who had been sexually abused as children themselves. They all opposed it.

"You'd be re-victimizing her," they said, "by invading her privacy."

I agreed. As a Rape Counselor put it to me: "If she's over 18 and hasn't tried to contact you, *she doesn't want to hear from you!*"

It may have been just as well, for when I looked deeper within myself what I found was that what I had really wanted to do wasn't just *apologize* to my daughter, but seek her forgiveness, and that's not her job to give. Finding it, if possible, is mine.

Perhaps, if I continue my work and she hears of it, she may choose to send me a signal that my approach would be welcome. And perhaps not. As I have written several prisoners with whom I now correspond, "not being forgiven may be part of the punishment we have drawn down upon ourselves. That doesn't mean it has to end there. While we may never attain forgiveness, this might help us to become more forgiving of others when they ask it of us."

What do you do, then, when you are left with a debt to pay and no one to pay it to? The answer was found by another man, three centuries ago in Japan. He was a notorious highwayman of that day who had robbed and killed many and, finally, on one moonlit night, as he looked down on the bodies of his newest victims, all the ugliness of his life stared back up at him and he saw it in full. He could continue it no further and began walking all the way to Tokyo to surrender himself.

Knowing that his execution would be immediate when he arrived there, the moment that he saw a small Buddhist temple outside of town, he thought to himself, "Since I will be meeting The Buddha today, I might as well do so with clean hands," and asked to see a priest so that he could make his confession.

An old monk was summoned and the man told him all that he had done and his intention now to surrender to the executioner. But, to his surprise, no forgiveness was granted. Only a question that the monk put to the man: "Why do you want to cheat the Buddha? By your own account, you have taken many lives. Now, you propose to pay for this by giving back only one: your own."

Startled, the man said, "But that's all that I have!"

"No," said the priest. "Instead of rushing to the executioner, you could stay here, train to become a monk and spend the rest of your days out on the highway saving others from men just like you. Then you could pay The Buddha back for all that you have taken."

The man did so, eventually becoming the "Saint Christopher" of Japan. It's a true story, and the one that guides what I do with my life now. When two local television news producers suggested I put my story in writing, I began this book again. Anxious that any success it enjoys not harm those still suffering from abuse—by me or by men like me—I asked a recent officer of the appropriate committee of the State Bar to guide me in making sure that any profits it earns go to appropriate purposes.

The lessons of this chapter, then, are that there are certain steps a convicted sex offender can take to earn his or her way back into the community. The following are the ones I've found. The next chapter tells of the steps that the community may take to make sure that any convicted offender living in its midst follows them.

The Ten Commandments for a Recovering Sex Offender

1. Overcome the Destructive Side of Yourself

We are people who have done terrible things. We have grievously injured many, some perhaps for the rest of their lives. If we do not grasp those facts—and do not have any feeling of sorrow for our victims—there is no way we can ever return to the community and be accepted by it. Remorse is the first step toward community reintegration.

That's not to say that we should bury ourselves in a shame so deep that it discourages us from believing that we can ever be anything other than what we have been. All too often, shame alone does nothing more than leave us wallowing in self-pity, which is useless.

Don't let your focus be on yourself, but on others and allow yourself to have a strong and permanent sense of abiding regret—not for what's happened to you, but to them because of you. For that regret, which others call remorse, will become the first wall in keeping you from ever harming anyone else again

See yourself now as you are: as a person instead of just as a person ruled by an urge. Be more than an 'offender.' Think of yourself, instead, as someone whose life has given them an enormous opportunity to become heroic by overcoming the destructive side of yourself.

Live like a warrior and tame yourself by respecting the power of your sexual urges. Never let yourself go into the world with urges that are still gathering power.

2. Choose your associates carefully so you aren't mentally contaminated by them.

We become part of everyone with whom we travel and the sum of every journey we take. Choose where you go carefully and with whom you wish to sojourn, for by the end of the journey each of you will be a part of the other.

If you allow yourself to fall back into the same old haunts and return to running around with the same kind of people to play the same old games as you did before you were convicted, it is as certain as tomorrow's sunrise that you will be convicted again.

Associate with people who inspire you to have a richer life.

3. Behave only as a guest in the community and not one of its equals. Respect not just its laws, but its sensitivities.

If you are a convicted rapist, don't believe that you have a 'right' to go to the same running trails that women use. If you are a convicted child molester, don't insist upon living right next door or in the same neighborhood where children play. If there's a park near your residence where children play, make a voluntary sacrifice and find another park for yourself.

This is not the time to test your new strength at the expense of the community's fears. For now, just content yourself with earning its toleration of your presence. Acceptance will come later. Don't try to force people into welcoming you by imposing yourself on them.

4. Practice self-disclosure about your past.

Don't be afraid to tell people about your past. You'll be thanked for doing so afterwards, if you do it humbly. Human beings are amazingly forgiving if you are willing to trust them and they are forever suspicious if they find out about you on their own.

You don't have to tell everyone. Just tell those who offer the hand of friendship. Any time you realize that a person is about to go from being an acquaintance to becoming a friend, ask them to pause a moment. Tell them how much you appreciate their company. Then, confess that, out of respect for them, there is something you must tell them that they have a right to know. Assure them that if, after they've heard it, they don't want to associate with you anymore, you'll accept that and respect their right not to do so.

Then, in the simplest possible terms, tell them about your past. For example: "A number of years ago (whenever) I did something that I regret very much. I (molested a child/forced a woman, etc). I've been convicted for it, as I should have been. Since that time, I've been in counseling (or

"I'm now in counseling") so that it never happens again. I regret it ever happened and I seek to live a much better life now. But I felt that you had a right to know about it. Thank you for hearing me out."

I have never yet been rejected by anyone to whom I have made such a disclosure and, instead, am able to count them as members of an ever-widening support group within my community that encourages my continued recovery.

You can do the same and never have to fear that others are going to find out about you on their own.

5. Respect the law: stay registered.

Registration protects us as well as the community. It keeps the community safe by letting others know who we are, and it keeps us safe by reminding us of who we have been so that we don't become it again.

Its alternatives are not better. Calls have already been heard, in this country and abroad, to have all convicted sex offenders confined in the same place, far away from the community, in special camps of their own from which they could never leave.

It's called preventative detention and it could be done. At the beginning of World War II, the United States forced over 100,000 of its Japanese-born American citizens into "relocation camps." Don't think it couldn't happen again.

You have the power to prevent that. Every time you walk into a police station to register or re-register, you are casting another vote against preventative detention by demonstrating that you are a law-abiding person who doesn't need to be confined.

6. Keep healing.

"...maintenance is forever."

> Marques, J.K., Murrey, C.L. and O'Connor, D.M., AN INNO-VATIVE TREATMENT PROGRAM FOR SEX OFFENDERS Report to the Legislature in Response to 1983/84 Budget Act Item 4440-011-001, State of California.

According to the most accurate figures currently available, therapy for sex offenders often wears off over time. This suggests that it's to our own benefit to remain in some kind of permanent maintenance program. A list of national and international organizations for sexual addicts that offers self-recovery programs appears below. Use them, or counseling programs equivalent to them. Consciousness is all we've got. Taking care of it is our highest calling.

7. Make amends to your victims except when doing so would harm them or others.

Unless they have made it clear that they do not wish to hear from you, have your former victims contacted through a trustworthy third party— e.g. your minister or legal representative—and given a letter of apology from you.

Leave it to your former victims to decide if they would then like to meet with you to discuss what happened in the past.

If they choose to permit a meeting with you, use a professional victim/offender mediator if you can (such as those available through the recognized organizations listed under Restorative Justice Resources below) so that the meeting may be one where the risk is minimal that either of you will be injured further by it.

Prepare yourself to express your regret, your sense of responsibility for what you did and your concern for your victim's future well being.

Do whatever you can to contribute to their further healing. But do not look to them to gain a forgiveness you can only earn by yourself by serving many others over a long period of time.

If your victim does not want to meet with you, leave them in peace for that is making amends to them too.

8. Cooperate with your community and work with your neighbors.

Be willing to participate in any community meeting about you to which you are invited and, when attending, be honest, polite and courteous in your responses to any questions you may be asked.

Understand that many people will be as afraid of you as you are of them. Be prepared to answer their concerns about you. Be open and willing to remain accountable to them whenever you encounter any of them in your daily life.

No matter how angry or hurt any of them may be (for some of them may also be former victims of sexual abuse by others), accept them as your guardians, for it is their watchfulness that will cause you to be watchful about yourself. And that is what will keep you out of prison.

9. Forgive anyone who has ever abused you and become a lamp of forgiveness to the entire community.

In every tragedy, life is always asking us one question: "Do you still love me?" Like it or not, life is our lover and if we will not forgive what she sometimes does to us her name is Hell.

Were I to meet-up again with the person who first molested me, I would neither sue nor prosecute him, for that would only make him a burden on his family.

I do not consider myself his "victim." I consider myself as having been the recipient of a damaging process that came through him after beginning a long, long time before he ever came into my life.

Were I to encounter him again, I would say nothing about our past unless he were now in a position to harm others, in which case I would then report him. For victims who only seek vengeance become abusers themselves and you cannot fix your own life by wrecking anyone else's.

10. Establish sexual government

Know what triggers your offending and outwit it. If you feel lonely, find the joy of being with yourself. If you are feeling low, ask yourself why you think your life should be the only one not to have any suffering in it.

Avoid situations of known temptation and have escape strategies in place when they occur. Accept as fact that urges to act inappropriately come to everyone. Don't fear such urges. All it takes to establish sexual government is remembering that, before there's an urge, there's a self to hear it.

Be that self. For, so long as you remain self-governing, no one else shall govern you.

*　　　　　*　　　　　*

Questions for Group Discussion

1. Johns Hopkins' Dr. Fred Berlin says that, since sex offenders don't choose their sexual inclinations any more than anyone else does, it isn't fair to 'blame' them, but it is fair to insist that they be responsible for governing them. What do you think?

2. What would be an appropriate occupation for a person previously convicted of a sexual offense? Someone convicted of rape? Of child molestation? Of indecent exposure? Or do you feel there is no job that such a person can ever be given again?

3. Should the victim of sexual abuse always be given the opportunity of receiving an apology from their abuser? If so, how should this be done without violating either the victim's privacy or feeling of safety from their former abuser?

4. Was it better that the former highwayman became a monk, spending the rest of his days saving others, or do you think that he just should have been executed?

5. Under what circumstances, if any, should a sex offender convicted of rape and/or child molestation be spared imprisonment? And, if so, ordered to do what, instead, to atone for their crime?

Chapter Ten

Establishing A Neighborhood Defense

According to two of the founders of modern-day sex offender therapy, more people find children erotically appealing than is widely acknowledged. Writing in their classic work, *Handbook of Sexual Assault*, Canada's W.L. Marshall and H.E. Barbaree suggest that at least *one out of every six men demonstrate significant levels of erotic arousal to girls as young as Age 13.*

Similarly, with regard to rape. According to one of the newest books on the subject, co-authored by a biologist and an anthropologist, *one out of every three college-age men admitted they would force a woman to have sex with them if they were certain that they could get away with it.* (Malamouth 1989; Young and Thiessen 1991, cited in Thornhill and Palmer, *A NATURAL HISTORY OF RAPE,* Cambridge 2000 at p. 77)

What these findings indicate is that there will always be sex offenders. They will continue to come forth in every generation. Locking them all up and throwing away the key is not the answer, for that would not reach those who have not yet been born. And when *they* come forth, knowing that's all you're going to do with them, the likelihood is that they will feel the same way that some already do now. As Sex Offender Psychologist Anna C. Salter writes of a typical serial rapist, "The threat of jail only made him consider killing his victim."

Any of them could become a *Man with Nothing Left to Lose* and that is a danger we dare not create when there are far-better alternatives. Children in danger of becoming sexual predators can be identified and helped before it's too late. Juveniles as well as adults who begin to offend can be given treatment to stop them. Those who have already become career sex offenders can be caught and prosecuted and treated while in prison.

Many have and many others have been sent to prison but released without being treated, leaving the final question one of what you can do to protect your self and your family before *any* convicted sex offender becomes a *repeat* sex offender living near you.

Neighborhood Guardians

The answer can be found right in your own home, in the neighborhood and in the community. There are steps you can take on any of four levels that can create a fortress of protection, ranging from using the new sex offender registration laws yourself to that of assisting local agencies in keeping convicted sex offenders in your community under watch. Choose the level that is most comfortable for you. Start there and master it. Once you've done so, you can advance to other levels whenever you feel ready to do so, or help others who are already there.

Level 1 is the use of the sex offender registration law to protect yourself and your loved ones simply by knowing who the convicted sex offenders are that are living nearby you, or are already in your lives closer than you think.

Level 2 is to join with your friends and neighbors to protect all of the children in your neighborhood.

Level 3 is where you can get more effective laws passed to protect you, which you can do right out of your own home from your desktop computer.

Level 4 is to help community corrections agencies keep convicted sex offenders on the mend or back in prison.

Level 1: Guarding Yourself and Your Loved Ones

The sex offender registration law is where you can begin, in many jurisdictions right on your computer. In the United States, go to any major search engine and type in the words "Megan's Law Registries" and scroll down until you see the Megan's Law registry for your state, and click on that. (Elsewhere, use the telephone and call your local police to ask them how to find a list of registered sex offenders living near you.) Directions will appear that guide you in looking up previously-convicted sex offenders and where they are living now. In many cases, you can also go to other state web sites to look up convicted offenders there.

With this law, you can—and should—check on anyone that you would:

- Date
- Marry
- Go into business with
- Work for
- Hire, or
- Use to take care of your children. (Even your relatives. Especially your relatives. Most sex offenses are committed by family members or people who are close to your child. If you have a nephew or uncle who has been convicted, he's not likely to tell you about it and it would be reckless for you to leave your child with him.)
- You can use it to look up new neighbors, for the safety of your family.
- As will be explained below, you can even use it to look up convicted sex offenders living anywhere, in other parts of your town or region.

The Supreme Court of the United States has now said that is everyone's constitutional right to look up convicted sex offenders. Use it to protect yourself. Don't wait for the police to come to your door and tell you that there's one living in your neighborhood now: police have too many doors to come to and by the time they get to yours it could be too late. It's your job to protect yourself and your children, and no one can do it better than you.

Remember, the sex offender registration law won't tell you who *all* the sex offenders are, only the ones who have been convicted, so keep your eye out for suspicious behavior by other people who are also around your children. The list of people registered won't tell you—and should—which of those who have been convicted have also had treatment and may be less dangerous. Most importantly, it won't—and can't—tell you who was really innocent and wrongly convicted but still has to register under it.

I've received several e-mails suggesting that's happened. One man told of how, after spending 67 days in a county jail awaiting trial where the conditions of confinement were so brutal that he would have admitted guilt to anything to get out, he accepted an offer from the prosecutor that let him go for time already served in exchange for admitting guilt to what he thought was a minor sexual offense. Now, he finds, he must register the rest of his life as a *convicted sex offender.*

The same thing happened to another man facing a prison sentence so horrendously long that he feared to take a chance and go through trial. He had a family to support and couldn't place them in jeopardy by risking such a fate.

Some people just lost their case! They weren't guilty. It's just that their attorney didn't do as well as the prosecutor. It happens in courtrooms all the time, in all kinds of cases.

That's not to say that everyone listed under the registration law is innocent, or even that most of them are not guilty. What it does say is that this list is just a start. Don't assume anything just because you've found someone who is on it. If the person is someone who is trying to get close to your family, tell them you found them listed on the sex offender registry and see what kind of a response they give you. In almost all cases, they'll simply admit it. If they admit and also insist they weren't guilty, you'll have to use your own judgment whether to trust them or not unless you go on to Level 4, where you can investigate the person's case yourself with the help of police or local community corrections agencies.

Level 2: Guarding the Neighborhood's Children

To guard not only your children, but all the children of your neighborhood:

1. Join with your friends and neighbors to act as Neighborhood Guardians, taking turns watching over each other's children when other parents or caregivers can not be at home with them.

2. Have a plan as to what any of you will do if a stranger comes into the neighborhood and appears to be bothering the children. Ask the police to help you form that plan, so you have it ahead of time. Don't wait until a threat surfaces to figure out what to do. Plan an

appropriate defense in advance and see to it that all the neighbors know what it is.

3. Tell the children, so they know who to go to for protection if a stranger comes into the neighborhood and is disturbing them. While a police officer can help you with additional suggestions, the children should be taught at least these simple rules:

Don't talk to strangers.

If a stranger approaches, stay away from them and ask them to leave you alone.

If the stranger doesn't leave you alone, run as fast as you can to the Neighborhood Guardian.

Level 3: How to Make A Sex Offender Registration Law More Effective

There are seven steps you can take to make sex offender registration laws stronger.

1. Keep this law to its original purpose.

There are people on some versions of these laws who don't belong there. As United States Supreme Court Justice David H. Souter said, upon reviewing Connecticut's version of Megan's Law:

> "The categories of individuals who are listed under the Connecticut statute include young men who as teenagers had intercourse with younger teenage girls. No one, by normal standards of English usage, would say at the age of 25 that—that a—young man like that is dangerous…(a)nd yet, there is no way for them, in effect, to—get themselves declared ineligible…"
>
> *Connecticut v. Doe, No. 01-1231,* IN THE SUPREME COURT OF THE UNITED STATES, November 13, 2002, Oral Argument of Petitioners, at 7 and 8, Alderson Reporting Company.

Some state versions require young men to register who did no more than have an affair with a girlfriend while he was just over age and she was still under age. Megan's Law wasn't created for that purpose. It was created to help parents protect their children from convicted *child sexual predators*: not from Romeo and Juliet.

Call the Registrar of Voters in your town and ask them to tell you who represents you in both houses of your state legislature and give you their local office's telephone number. Call either of your representatives in state government and ask their staff to tell you if young people found guilty of *statutory* rape (where the conduct was consensual, but one party was under age and the other was over the age of consent) must be registered. If they are, bring this to the attention of your fellow Neighborhood Guardians so that everyone can discuss it. If they agree that such a requirement is unfair or unnecessary, adopt a resolution among yourselves to that effect and send it to your state legislators and ask them to repeal that part of the law.

Send a copy to the local newspaper and radio and television stations.

If you receive a reply from your legislators that they will help you change the law, ask when they will act, and how you can track the move to repeal on your computer. All states have a website you can access to watch as a bill moves on to passage. The office of your state legislators can tell you where to find it.

Check that website regularly. When the measure is going before a committee, you can use the website to find the name and office address of each member of that committee. Write them and tell them what you want them to do. Tell the legislator who is seeking its repeal for you and your fellow Neighborhood Guardians that you are willing to tell the committee how its members feel. If your offer is accepted, go there and politely explain those views and you will find they are appreciated. It's your government and you have a right to be heard.

Let every legislator you contact know that you and your organization will remember them at voting time.

Thank them for their help, no matter how their efforts end.

Watch the news and remain aware. Whenever you learn that another move is going to be made to add anyone convicted of some additional offense, have your Neighborhood Guardians discuss it. If you favor it, let your legislators know that. And if you don't, let them know that too.

2. Keep the Rules of Sex Offender Registration Laws Up to Date

In many parts of the United States, anyone listed under Megan's Law has to register all over again, *anytime* they go to another city or county, even for a short visit. (One day in Alaska.) Worse, when they return, they have to register all over again right where they started, just as if they were moving-in anew. When I went to a neighboring county for a week to go on retreat with my fellow Buddhists and take vows, I had to register in that county and then again in my own when I returned, *even though I'd already paid rent on my apartment for the whole month!*

Twice, police had to take time from other duties to do paperwork on me that could have been avoided.

The reason for this requirement may be found by reading virtually any state's registration statute. They're all based on a political myth—that everyone convicted of a sex offense, no matter how long ago, is part of a restless, roaming band of *predators* who do nothing but migrate from community-to-community, like scavengers seeking new victims. This completely ignores the fact that most of us hold jobs and pay rent or make mortgage payments and have neither the time nor the money to live on the road.

Can you imagine how irksome it is to be made to re-register in another county or state as a "permanent registrant" (the only category they offer) even if you are only staying for a few days on business or to visit your family? And, then, when you return home, being made to register AGAIN, as if you had just become a "permanent registrant" there, too? My own city's police complained to me about this law when I came back from taking vows, and I can't print the words they used!

The answer is to change the law so that anyone who is already registered doesn't have to register again if they are only going to be absent from their residence temporarily (thirty days or less), so long as they return there before the end of that period as that is when most people's next rent or mortgage payment is due anyhow.

Police may complain that they won't know when such a person is visiting in their community. But that kind of concern was only fueled by the earlier belief that those already convicted of sex offenses have a high re-offense rate. More recent figures show that to be untrue and the law should be changed accordingly, as over 90% of these people remain re-offense free. When nine out of ten are not going to re-offend anyhow, there is no need for them to report to police in every place they are only visiting before they go back home again, taking police away from other duties that are also calling them.

Leave the police free to do police things. The normal registrant only needs to be *seen* in the police station once a year: to make certain that he hasn't altered his appearance so much that a new photo has to be taken. At all other times, police should be spared from being taken away from all the other work it has to do to protect you.

If your fellow Neighborhood Guardians agree that this is a worthwhile reform, draft a resolution to that effect and send it to your state legislator. Tell him or her that you'd like the law changed so that police don't have to register people who are only going to be away from their homes for thirty days or less, so police can remain free to do other more pressing tasks.

Go to your computer and log in to: www.naag.org to reach the website for the National Association of (State) Attorneys General. On the home page for this organization, you will see a box that says: "Find Your Attorney General." Below it, there's a drop-down menu. Simply click on the tab for your state and a page listing your state's attorney general will appear. At the bottom of that attorney general's page, you will find that official's phone number and office address. Send a copy of the resolution that your Neighborhood Guardians group has drafted to this official and ask him or her to support it.

Follow up on any response that officials give you so that you can see your efforts succeed: watch each part of the process. With your help, we could have a system that's more accurate than one that now falsely lists people as if they've moved away when they've only gone to see their family or left for a few days on business. That's why so many registries are not completely accurate and this is how to help end that so the list is kept up-to-date.

3. Have the Sex Offender Registry use Ordinary Language, and not just legal terms.

A registry that tells you that I was convicted of two counts of violating "Section 288 (a) of the California Penal Code" doesn't give you a clue as to what I did that got me sent to prison, unless you're a lawyer and have a copy of my state's penal code handy. It doesn't tell you *anything* you can use to know whether I am dangerous to you or your children. It requires you to *hire an attorney* to explain it to you, and when the people can't understand the law, they can't use the law.

Write your legislator and tell him or her that you want a sex offender registry that tells you *in everyday language* what the person has done, just like I use on my Web site to discuss the law with my fellow sex offenders. Next to every section number from the penal code I use *plain* language: "child molestation," "rape," words like those, so that the reader who doesn't have a law degree can understand what the law says.

Tell your legislature that you want a registry that the people can understand.

Also tell them that you want it to be *honest.* It's needlessly alarmist to call a person who registers anything but a "registrant." To call them a "sex offender" suggests they still are actively breaking the law, when that cannot be assumed. Only the police would know if that person is still an active *sex offender* and, if so, they wouldn't be on the list: they'd be in jail. Anyone who comes under the registration law is only a *registrant* and should not be called anything else until proven guilty. Making one's way back after such a conviction is hard-enough, without being spoken of as if you were still committing it the rest of your life. The public should not be misled or needlessly alarmed.

Similarly, when the law uses the words "violent" or "rape." Those are *important* words: they let you know how much caution you should take with a person to whom those words apply. And they needlessly *waste* your concern over people who don't deserve them.

Many jurisdictions call it "rape" when *no* forcible sexual act has occurred at all. Instead, they simply call an act *rape* when the person who was touched inappropriately was a minor. That's not *rape.* That's *child molestation.*

Similarly, many call it "violent" if a child is only touched. Mere touching is *not* violent. It may be lewd, it may be wrong, it may be impermissible. But the public cannot be adequately warned of truly-violent people who have engaged in truly violent behavior if the word "violent" is misused so much that, like the boy who cried 'wolf!' it is finally ignored.

Call for a rewrite of the registration law that will use words like the dictionary does. We need a law we can fully trust. You and your fellow Neighborhood Guardians could help create one. Discuss the idea with them and if they agree, contact your representatives in government and tell them you and your fellow Neighborhood Guardians want it done.

4. Demand a Sentencing System that Works.

Every person who commits a sex offense should go to jail and have appropriate sex offender therapy offered to them. They should not leave jail until they have been given enough treatment to be safe to be released.

Too many times, they are merely put away (five years is the average sentence) and then released *no better than they were when they went in.*

That is inviting disaster.

Treatment should not wait, as it does in some jurisdictions, until after they have finished serving their prison sentence: that could be years, when their memory of the offense they committed is so dimmed that they can no longer accurately remember it. Besides, at $20,000 a year to keep them in jail, it's a waste of your money when they could be treated and then returned to the community under continuing supervision, and work to pay for the damage they've caused instead of making you work to support their remaining in prison.

Treatment should start on Day One of their imprisonment.

A prison chaplain should be made available to every sex offender who wants to use one. *Adding a spiritual dimension to recovery strengthens it enormously.*

Sentences shouldn't stop with prison. Every convicted sex offender who returns to the community should be required to do *community service* as part of his payment to society for having damaged it. All but those deemed sadistic offenders should be required to appear before Victims Groups so that they can tell him how much damage his kind of acts really caused. Very few offenders ever find out. Is it any wonder that they haven't any remorse? They've never seen any of the long-term *consequences* of what they've done and should be made to do so.

Demand these changes. Tell your state legislators that you want sex offenders given treatment while they are confined, kept there until they have completed it, provided with the services of a chaplain if they wish and made to do community service when they get out, with treatment starting the moment they go into custody.

Critics may complain that all of this will cost too much money. But when it's measured against the cost of more victims if the offender isn't treated and gets back out again, that argument is unacceptable. Every time that a sex offender is sent to prison without treatment, it is the community that is sentenced.

5. Trust the Treatment Professionals

The decision to release a convicted sex offender should not be made by anyone but professionals. In some jurisdictions, under civil commitment programs, a *jury* decides whether they are to be kept in a mental hospital after they have served their prison time or be released.

A jury should *never* be burdened with making such a decision. Even if you felt that it was the right thing to do, and the man was ready to come back out, how could you come home and tell your neighbors that "Today, I let a man out who was convicted twenty years ago of raping five people." Your neighbors would hang you!

Such a decision is too dangerous to ask that a lay person make it. And those who have gone through treatment and become self-controlled again *deserve* the right to come home. Don't think, for one moment, that doctors can't tell if we're *safe* to be released. The old days of laying back on some doctor's couch and talking for hours aren't used in most jurisdictions. There's a new device that can *read our sexual impulses* no matter how hard we try to hide them. It's like a Sexual Lie Detector and I voluntarily put myself under it a few years ago at a clinic in the southwestern part of the United States, just to see if it worked.

It acted like a wake-up call to me! I had no idea how powerful some of my more hidden urges were, and that made me become even more vigilant, which is what it should do. With devices like that, treatment professionals today can tell if a person has really changed or not. Their decisions deserve to be trusted if they use that technology.

Yes, mistakes may still be made. No matter how careful people may be, sooner or later, someone is going to get out who shouldn't have been released. But the alternative is worse: if we aren't willing to let *anyone* out, we're right back where we were at the start of this book, making every sex offender into a *Man With Nothing Left to Lose* until he's caught, and we dare not do that as it's too dangerous for public safety. We have to give people a chance to come back, and we have to trust our corrections and treatment professionals to know when it's safe for them to do so, or we risk making every child molester into a child killer and that is not the answer.

6. Let Judges Determine Punishments, not Politicians.

For too many years now, politicians have tried to say that "judges are too lenient." As a result, many laws have been passed that tie a judge's hands and force the court to hand down a sentence written in advance in a law book (as *mandatory minimums*). Every individual deserves to be judged solely on the basis of his own case. The alternative is lynch mob justice and that only serves to make criminals more violent.

Courts were created so that their judges could restrain us from letting our own passions—instead of wisdom—govern. They were made independent so they could even restrain the legislature from acting excessively. They were created as the guardians of our reason. Don't let politicians who appeal only to anger or rage determine what justice is to be or we will be devoured by violence.

Let judges judge. Call some of them up and ask to meet them in court with your fellow Neighborhood Guardians during a recess. Have them tell you what they think should be done in sex offense cases. You may be surprised at the variety of opinions they have.

If you are satisfied with what you've heard, have your Neighborhood Guardians group use e-mail to tell its local and national legislators that *you want judges left free to judge.* If you don't like what a judge does, you can always elect another.

You can't do that with a law book. Government is best when it remains changeable by the people. Don't give up your right to control your own courts. And don't let the courts be deprived of their power, for it is only by keeping the executive, lawmaking and judicial powers independent of each other that the people are protected from any one of those powers dominating the others and then dominating the people themselves.

7. Protect and Defend the Sex Offender Registration Law

This law is here to protect you. In turn, it also needs your protection. As you will see below, there are those in the United States who mean to burden former offenders with so many restrictions as to make it impossible for them to live in many cities and states. This could force them to choose between staying registered or finding shelter and work while living secretly among their neighbors once again. That could cause Megan's Law to collapse as that would take away the public's ability to know who we are.

These new restrictions on lawfully registered former offenders are not good laws.

- **The United States Department of Housing and Urban Development** has announced that it intends to deny housing to *anyone* whose household will include *any member or relative* registered under Megan's Law. (HUD Directive Number 5.856) That means a recovering sex offender can't even go visit his own family without making it lose their housing if it was given to them by HUD. That is rank discrimination and wrongful. People convicted of sex offenses—and their families—pay taxes to support federally assisted housing, like everyone else. A conviction is no reason to deny them housing. As the United States Supreme Court recognized, the fact that someone is registered for having been convicted of a sex offense does not mean they will commit it again. All this regulation does is discourage people from registering and that means it endangers Megan's Law.

- **New Mexico:** the Governor of New Mexico has announced that he intends to fire anyone convicted of a sex offense from state employment, no matter how long ago the person was convicted: even if the job is no more than that of being a highway maintenance worker out on the road. As one parole agent said to me, "What do they think the man is going to do: grab a child out of a car going 65 miles per hour?" If we pay taxes like anyone else, why can't we have a job if no child will be placed in danger by our performing it?

- Over one-quarter of the States have now created so-called *child safety zones* that bar *lawfully-registered sex offenders* from working or living anywhere near a city school, playground, park or child care facility, instead of just forbidding us from being on their premises.

- Excluded from these areas of the cities, many of our kind have begun to live close to each other, in the most run-down neighborhoods or, in even worse cases, on the ragged edges of the countryside where some among us have begun to angrily brood.

- Seven states—**Alabama, Florida, Illinois, Iowa, Kentucky, Louisiana and Oregon**—now have measures on their books prohibiting registered sex offenders from residing anywhere within 500 to 2000 feet of many sites where children gather. In Alabama and Louisiana, registrants are also forbidden to hold jobs in such areas, creating *apartheid* zones excluding them when it is hard to find work anywhere else.

- Seven other states are considering joining them. **Arkansas, Georgia, Missouri, Oklahoma, Ohio, Tennessee and Wisconsin** now have legislation pending that would bar many registered sex offenders from working or living within those same zones that surround every elementary or secondary school, daycare or childcare facility, playground or educational institution. Oklahoma's law would even apply to out-of-state registrants passing through or only visiting, even on the job, making work impossible for them in many instances.

Lawsuits in state and federal courts, challenging the measures already in force in Iowa, Alabama and in the city of Albuquerque, New Mexico, have now been filed, alleging that these laws unconstitutionally *punish* those of us who have already served our sentences. Also, that they fail to provide clear-enough notice to let us know exactly *where* these so-called child safety zones begin and end, so that we do not enter them *by accident*.

If these new laws are allowed to drive lawfully-registered sex offenders out of the cities, we could easily see them become an angry band of exiled sexual predators roaming across the countryside and that could threaten public safety everywhere. A far wiser approach would simply be to make certain every convicted sex offender is given four things:

- adequate training in prison to make them fully aware of the community's needs before they get out, so they stay away from places where children gather,
- adequate supervision when they first return to the community, to keep them from going there,
- loitering and trespass laws that keep them off a forbidden *site*, instead of banned from its surroundings altogether, and
- adequate training for our children so that they promptly report all suspicious strangers to their teacher or child care supervisor who can then call police to investigate.

It's tempting to suggest that a law be passed, forbidding anyone convicted of a sex offense against a child from living in a *neighborhood* where there are children. But such a law might also apply to any young boy in your family who gets in trouble for becoming sexually involved with his girl friend under the new statutory rape laws, for in some jurisdictions those offenses would also make him into a *registered sex offender*. Does anyone really think such a boy would remain a danger to all other children *for the rest of his life?*

What we need is a fair balance. Banning those who have paid their debt to society from entire *zones* of a city is not the answer. Forbidding them from being on the *grounds* of schools, playgrounds and daycare centers is enough.

Equally, there is no wisdom in driving lawfully-registered sex offenders—who are harming no one—out of your community. For if you drive them out of your community, other communities will start doing the same and soon you'll just be trading sex offenders with each other. And when the new ones come in after having been driven out for being registered, *they may not register again.*

It's far wiser to keep the devil you've got than to trade him for the one you don't know.

Your Neighborhood Guardians group could help by making its voice heard. Stay aware of the news. Whenever you find that an unfair law is being proposed, oppose it. Whenever you find that such a law is in force, all you have to do is send a letter or e-mail to the Attorney General of your state, asking that he take legal action to halt it.

Send a copy by e-mail to your state legislator and the Governor.

Send a copy to the local radio and television stations and the newspapers. Write a letter to the editor.

Don't let alarmist politicians fool you into thinking that they are 'tough on crime' because they are going to make things harder for people who have already paid for their crime.

Anything that needlessly discourages a person already in recovery only threatens to push him or her out of recovery, and that endangers your family. We can't afford it.

*   *   *

Questions for Group Discussion

1. Do you think that judges should be left free to determine criminal sentences?

2. Would you favor a law forbidding convicted sex offenders from living in a family neighborhood? If so, what should be done when families with children move into a neighborhood in which a convicted person already resides?

3. How many years would have to pass before you felt that a convicted sex offender could live near you? If your answer is "never," would you impose the same rule on other criminals who also hurt people, sometimes for life, like the holdup artist whose bullet left a store owner crippled?

4. Should juveniles who have committed sexual offenses also be publicly listed on sex offender registration websites?

5. Would you feel differently if you had a daughter who could be dating one of them?

Chapter Eleven

How To Prevent Tomorrow's Crimes

This is where you can take control. This is Level 4 participation. When you are willing to do so, you can have a direct say over how sex offenders living in your community are handled. To do so effectively, here are the things that you need to know.

Not all sex offenders are as dangerous as those who get all the publicity.

A recent portrait compiled by the Minnesota Department of Corrections suggests that the public holds a highly-exaggerated image as to how dangerous most sex offenders really are. Looking over its records, it found that the typical *victim* of sexual assault is a female under the age of 18 years who is usually an acquaintance or relative of the offender's.

Half the time she turns out to have been living with him. The most common injuries sustained by her are emotional and not physical. While this is not to dismiss these as inconsequential, the fact is that she is more often a victim of deception than of physical brutality.

As the Minnesota report found, "Victim compliance was achieved in numerous ways, the majority of which did *not* involve the use of force or infliction of physical injury." (Italics added for emphasis.)

A later report issued by the Association for the Treatment of Sexual Abusers, the nation's leading organization of clinicians in this field, finds no ground for viewing *all* sex offenders as dangerous. Instead, it writes, there is "significant variation" among them as to the likelihood of their re-offending; **it is a "misconception that *all* sex offenders are highly likely to commit new sex offenses, and…most sex offenses against children are committed, not by strangers, but by *family members and others the child knows and trusts.***"

British police echo those same findings:

Within the UK, all research and crime statistics reveal that in excess of 80% of sexual offences committed against children are perpetrated by family members of the child.

In approximately 10-12% of other cases the offender was known to the child and occupied a position of trust, ie a member of the clergy, a teacher, a sports coach, etc.

In only 1 or 2% of cases is the child abused or attacked by someone unknown to them...

—Letter to Mr. R.J. Goldenflame, JD MA, dated 13 September 1999
Inspector Ian P. Clark, Staff Officer to the Chief Constable,
Gloucestershire Constabulary, England.

While it cannot be denied that there are some truly dangerous sex offenders, according to a top expert in the field, they are estimated as being no more than 2 to 5 percent of all sex offenders. (Anna C. Salter, *PREDATORS: Pedophiles, Rapists and Other Sex Offenders* (New York, 2003). P. 97.)

A Model Program for Preventing Repeat Sex Offenders Exists

It was created almost a decade ago in Canada, when the Mennonite religious order decided to help heal sex offenders themselves. Taking their stand in Radical Christianity, they said that if, in His time, Jesus healed lepers (the social outcasts of His era), Christians should help heal sex offenders today.

Their first attempt to do so was with a high-risk 54-year old child molester about to leave prison after his eighth conviction. They met with his caseworker, agreed to help the man find a place to stay, a job and build a new circle of friends who would support his living a new life. Then they contacted the police to let them know of their involvement.

Detectives were not overjoyed at the news. "We didn't want him here."

The moment he arrived at the Mennonite facility, his picture was quickly made available to the media and the public warned of his presence.

Irate parents began picketing outside and the Mennonites received so many angry phone calls that, for the first time in their lives, they had to buy a telephone answering machine.

The police intensified their surveillance, certain the man would quickly re-offend.

A neighbor phoned, who had small children and was very concerned for their safety. They invited her to come over and tell the man her fears so that he could speak to them. Several other neighbors were also invited, as were the police.

Ground rules were quickly established. Everyone would sit in a circle and speak one-at-a-time, followed by an opportunity for the man to respond. He was asked a number of questions:

- why had he been in prison?
- what was his sentence?
- what treatment had he obtained?
- what treatment did he plan to get now that he was out of prison?

Other participants asked him the best way he had learned to avoid repeating his misconduct, and how he planned to deal with the anger that some people might feel toward him.

He answered each question fully and respectfully and tensions began to ease.

A program was set up by which he would be contacted every day by at least one member of a small group of Mennonite volunteers who would check on how he was doing. He was given help in finding furniture and an apartment while police met regularly with the organization and began acting as a buffer between the man and the community, correcting rumors and preventing problems.

The man's life soon settled into a comfortable pattern as he took up residence in his own apartment and developed some close relationships among a small network of people willing to encourage him in remaining self-controlled.

As a result of this experience, the Mennonites found themselves with a model they could use with other men like him and now do so regularly. Each man works with a small group of volunteers who agree to help for one year and learn about sexual deviation, its damage to victims and the prospects for recovery by both victim and offender, consulting with professionals whenever possible.

A formal agreement is set up between the man and his group by which he agrees to accept their help and advice, pursue appropriate treatment and act responsibly in the community. In return, volunteers agree to help him. Procedures are established for failure to live up to these commitments, with consequences that can include adjustment of terms or, when necessary, withdrawal of support and notification of authorities.

Former victims who have processed their experience well are also invited to some meetings so that their needs and views are addressed, too.

First statistics on the program's results show that these men do twice as well as men who are not in this program and that, when new crimes are committed by them, they are substantially less severe than the offense for which they had previously been imprisoned.

Says one Canadian Correctional Services official:

"I fundamentally believe sex offenders are a problem of the community that needs to be addressed by the community. If you wait for politicians and government bureaucrats to do it, there are going to be far too many abused children because there aren't enough of us."

> Robin J. Wilson, director of the Sexual Behavior Program, Canadian Correctional Service, quoted by Journalist Candis McLean in her article "Next step—a national registry," REPORT NEWS-MAGAZINE, June 3, 2002, Alberta, Canada

An 8-Step Path to Neighborhood Safety

Many of the methods that work for the Mennonites could be adapted by your neighborhood. But this should be done only because you want to do so, not because I have suggested it or anyone else, as no liability is assumed. Like the Mennonites, your work should be done only in conjunction with local corrections agencies and your police department. This is not vigilante work, or organizing a private posse. People who try and do it on their own could get seriously hurt and are urged *not* to do so. People who have been victims of sexual assault should ask their therapist if they are ready to do this kind of work before they attempt it.

This is for neighborhood residents ready to become Neighborhood Guardians in the fullest sense of that term. It requires dedication but could vastly improve your neighborhood's safety. This is an idea of what you could do today:

Step One. Have your Neighborhood Guardians group use the sex offender registration law to learn the identity and location of every registered sex offender living nearby. If your state doesn't display them that way on its registry, tell them that they should. The sheriff of Corpus Christi, Texas does: his department uses a Sex Offender/Child Predator Search engine that allows residents to view a map on their own home computer any time they want, showing every registered sex offender within a mile of them—instead of merely within an entire Zip code or list for the whole state. If your state registry doesn't have such a system, write your governor and insist that they get one.

If your state's registry doesn't tell you the following facts, phone the police and ask them to help you learn:

- the crime(s) for which each person was convicted, in plain language,
- their relationship with their victim: was that person a stranger to them or someone they knew?
- the method they used to obtain their victim(s),
- the sentence they served and when (as it is likely, even if not certain, that the person who has been out of prison for years without having any more problems is probably not going to be as dangerous as someone who has only been out a few weeks),
- whether they are under supervision in the community now and, if so,
- the name and office phone number of their community supervisor.

Step Two. *If they are under supervision in the community*, call their supervisor and invite that official *and the registered offender* to a meeting of your Neighborhood Guardians so that you can tell the registrant your concerns and you can learn his. Together, you could form an agreement like the Mennonites did as to what is expected of him and what he can expect from you and your group by way of monitoring as well as support.

Step Three. *Ask the community supervising official to work with you.* Do not take any further steps until such an official knows what you plan to do. Sex offenders, as I showed you when describing my worst years, are often very deceptive people. We've spent our whole lives deceiving ourselves and, from that, deceive everyone else until we've been through a lot of training to become more honest. You shouldn't trust them. You should rely on police or community corrections people to guide you in working with them.

Seek additional assistance from the mental health profession by contacting a member who has experience in dealing with sex offenders. If none is available, contact the Department of Psychology at your nearest university and ask them to find someone to help you understand sex offenders better. Use any of the referral organizations listed in the back of this book to learn which professionals may be closest to your community and consider drawing upon them for assistance.

Step Four. *Assemble several of your members to work with the community supervisor and the convicted offender to check on how he is doing,* by phone, every day for the first six months, then once a week for the rest of the first year. Invite the registered offender and that community supervisor to future meetings on at least a monthly basis so that your neighbors can continue to encourage the registrant—and he can continue to learn what they require of him.

If you ever feel that he is in danger of re-offending, let his community supervisor, or the police, know immediately. They'll investigate; that's their job.

Step Five. *If the person is not under community supervision,* organize a delegation from among your fellow Neighborhood Guardians and *ask the police to go with them* to the offender's residence and tell him:

- We know who you are
- We wish you well in your continuing recovery
- We offer to help you succeed by inviting you to a neighborhood meeting we are having, to get to know you better and to let you get to know us.

If the reason that the person is not under community supervision is because he or she has already completed it, those steps may be enough as such a person has already had supervision and shown an ability to stay self-controlled. He should just be left welcome to attend your meetings whenever he wishes to do so.

But if the person is not under community supervision because there is no such program in your jurisdiction, find out from police how long he has been out of jail. If it is less than three years, do the same things listed above for those who are under community supervision, using the police as you would have used a community supervisor to guide you: in checking in with him daily, having him at meetings, and remaining aware of what is going on with him and how he is progressing.

If he has been out of prison or jail for *more than three years,* your just having met him and introduced yourself may be enough to let him know that others are aware of him.

Step Six. *If the police tell you that anyone is too dangerous to approach, do not do so* but get the name of whoever is in charge of that police station and make an appointment to see that official with members of your Neighborhood Guardian organization. When you meet with that officer, ask to be told what the station is willing to do to keep that individual under constant surveillance. Ask the police to give you copies of that person's photograph and distribute it among your neighbors. Write that registered offender a letter and tell him:

- We know who you are.
- We wish you well, but have been told you are too dangerous to approach.
- We urge you to join a counseling program for sex offenders immediately.
- If you do so, and have your counselor send us a note confirming that you are in treatment, we will work with that person and you so that you have a good life here.
- If you do not send us such a note within thirty days, we will do everything we can to see that you are placed in a counseling program at the earliest opportunity.

Have the police deliver it to him and tell you his response. Unless it's favorable and you learn that he has entered a treatment program, stay away from him.

Step Seven. *If he enters a treatment program,* get proof and then ask him to come to a meeting where a member of the police or his community supervisor will also be present, for he is on the mend and you could form a group to help encourage him, under the guidance of these officials. But *never work with this kind of person alone,* only with law enforcement or community corrections people present.

Step Eight. *If he does not enter a treatment program,* contact the police regularly to make certain they are keeping him under tight surveillance. Tell the local news people about your group's concerns, so they can bring these to the attention of the rest of the community and check back regularly with the authorities to learn how they are handling the matter. You are making the community a safer one.

A Partnership in Healing

Standing in the realization that sex offending is not curable—that it can be managed but not cured—the challenge is to keep it managed so that it does not occur again. What Megan's Law (or any of the other sex offender registration laws in other countries) is out to do is stop repeat sex offending.

What it offers to those who will accept it is a *partnership in healing*: between offenders who voluntarily walk into police stations and register as required, and the community in which they do so. If the community will use the information provided by the registration law to monitor the sex offender, and the offender will accept the members of his community as his guardians, the community's children will remain safe and the former offender will be able to have a life in which he can be more than just a slave to his urges; he can become a person again.

Far too frequently, public discussion on the subject of sex offender registration laws has been driven either by alarmists or apologists, pleading that those of us who have committed sex offenses deserve to be 'left alone' now as we have *paid for our crimes.*

Some crimes can't be paid for: all that can be done is to make certain they don't happen again. This we can do, working together. This we must do for those who have already been injured. No one wants to spare others more than they do. Let us respect their determination to be the final victims.

If you will form a neighborhood group and use this law to reach out to former offenders and let them know what is expected of them—and report them when they fail while encouraging them when they give it—you will fully realize the promise of this law. For the final truth about sex offenders and the community is that neither is healed until both are healed.

I say, to all of you, that together we can end the terror that divides us and be reunited as a people once again—only this time, more honestly.

*   *   *

Questions for Group Discussion

1. How do you feel about the job that the authorities are doing with sex offenders in your community?

2. How would you feel about having religious congregations follow the Mennonite Program in working with sex offenders? Would you be willing to tell them about it?

3. Would you be willing to help community corrections officials, like parole agents and/or probation officers, in monitoring sex offenders living nearby?

4. What difficulties do you think you would find in speaking to a sex offender? What would you need to hear from him or her before you could feel comfortable in having such a person in your midst?

5. Do you think that you could participate in a Neighborhood Guardian program?

Chapter Twelve

Summary: How to Protect Your Children from Sexual Predators

You can't protect your children against sexual predators alone. It can't be done. It takes your child's help, too. Although no argument is made against the proposition that the child victim of a sexual offense is never to *blame* for it, we have to remember that the word *blame* is a legal concept: used in a court of law to say who shall be punished. Clearly, no child deserves to be *punished* by the law for having been victimized by a sexual offender.

But that doesn't mean that older children, in particular, can't be asked to assume some responsibility for what happens to them. To allow a girl in her young teens to go out and flirt without limits with adult men does not protect her. To allow your young son to go out and join anyone they've just met on the Internet does not protect him. As children grow up, their capability for taking on a greater role in protecting themselves should be encouraged and not dismissed as unimportant. When child protection advocates insist "the child is never to blame," that should not be misunderstood to mean that children get to have a free ride sexually with anyone they meet.

Yet, increasingly, today's children don't seem to be given any values to live by except that of seeing life as a place to have fun and feel good. If you really want your child to be safe from sexual predators, teach your children self-respect and teach your child to live with a set of sensible limits that you give them and demonstrate in your own life.

Those are the first steps to protecting your children. Everything else in this book comes second, and won't work if your children don't also do their part.

Here's a summary of what this book suggests can also be done:

To protect your child from predators on the Internet or in the street (Chapter 2)

- Teach your children never to have conversations with strangers about the child's own sexual interests and urges: on the Internet, in chat rooms or on the street.
- Teach your child that the only proper reply to a question from a stranger about the child's sexual interests is "Goodbye."
- Hitchhiking is dangerous. It could cost your child their life. Hitchhiking at night is even more dangerous, or near secluded areas. A child should never seek or accept a ride from a stranger.
- Hitchhiking on the Internet is just as dangerous and, all that often, that's all a child is doing when they go into a Chat Room full of unknown people. Teach your child that, on the Internet with strangers, no one can ever know if the person they are exchanging messages with really is who they claim to be. Tell your child never to meet such a person alone or they may not come home.

To protect your child from adult predators in youth groups (Chapter 2)

There are signs you can use that may tell you that your child will be *safe* with adults in charge there:

- one sign is the man who also always has a woman present, and vice versa;
- another is that he always has other kids around at the same time, and
- a third is that he never takes any child anywhere, alone.

To rescue the child who is already being sexually abused (Chapter 2)

If your child tells you that he or she has had any experience with an adult or older child that made your child feel uncomfortable:

- Stay calm. Do not allow yourself to panic or react in anger.
- Assure the child that it wasn't the child's fault and that they did the right thing in telling you, because you will see to it that it never happens again.

- Phone a lawyer for help in contacting the appropriate agencies for assistance so that the child is not abused further, as you probably aren't going to be settled enough to do this correctly on your own.

To prevent a sexually abused child from growing up to become a child abuser (Chapter 2)

- Use any of the national referral organizations for abused children listed under the Readers Resources section in the back of this book and take the child to a clinician for help.

To prevent child prostitution (Chapter 3)

- Contact *Children of the Night*, a private, non-profit, tax-exempt organization formed to combat the abuse of children on the street by pimps and pedophiles. Tele: 1-800-551-1300 or visit their website at *http://childrenofthenight.org*
If you live outside of the United States, call your local police and ask them to tell you who does the same thing and help them.

To prevent incest (Chapter 3)

- If you see a marriage in trouble where there are children, urge its members to get professional counseling and restore it to health, or end it as amicably as possible so the child doesn't become its next casualty.
- If you find yourself in such a marriage, do the same so that the child doesn't become its next casualty.
- If you want parents who you suspect are already trapped in incest to be able to get professional help—to save the child from further molestation—tell your state legislators that you want the law changed so that no parent who comes to an appropriate clinician or counselor for help after the first time they lose control is given a prison sentence, unless there was also physical brutality.

To prevent repeat sex offenders (Chapters 4, 5, 6, 7 & 8)

Tell your lawmakers that you want every sex offender:

- sent to prison and given professional treatment
- kept there until their treatment team feels they are safe for release
- monitored when they are released, and
- returned to prison if they fail to stay safe to have back in the community.
- Tell your lawmakers that you want sex offenders in prisons placed in special yards where they can safely get treatment without fearing that they will be harmed for being known as convicted sex offenders.
- Tell your lawmakers not to punish those in prison who admit to other crimes while in treatment, so that treatment is sought fully. Laws seeking vengeance for previously unknown crimes only endanger public safety as they discourage offenders from seeking treatment.
- Tell your lawmakers that you want every convicted sex offender to be given training in how addictions may be controlled, as sex offending is often controllable the same way.
- Beware the public alarmist who insists that nothing can be done except vote for him to make laws even tougher. That's not solving the problem, that's turning it into a *war* where children are the casualties.
- Don't ask a convicted sex offender that you think is cured to take on any role that common sense tells you he or she should not be given again: such as acting as your child's baby sitter.
- Don't believe that deliberately making return to the community difficult for the lawfully-registered sex offender is the answer. Anything that discourages a former sex offender from staying in recovery only encourages him to give up on staying in recovery.
- Tell your lawmakers that you want every convicted sex offender to do some community service when he or she returns, e.g. by working with sexual abuse victim survivors groups. Offenders who see the long-term damage and meet the people who have been damaged are less likely to damage anyone else again.

To guard against possible repeat sex offenders who move in near you (Chapters 9 & 10)

Use your jurisdiction's sex offender registry (Megan's Law or its equivalent) to look up anyone you would:

- Date
- Marry
- Go into business with
- Work for
- Hire or
- Use to take care of your children.
- Use it to see if any convicted sex offenders are living nearby you.
- Join with your friends and neighbors to act as Neighborhood Guardians, taking turns watching over each other's children when their parent or caregiver cannot be at home.
- Have a plan as to what any of you will do if a stranger comes into the neighborhood and appears to be bothering any of the children. Ask the police to help you form that plan so that you have it ahead of time.
- Teach the children who they should go to for help when you cannot be at home.
- Keep the Sex Offender Registration Law efficient by not requiring re-registrations from people on it who are only going to be gone from their normal residence for 30 days or less.
- Insist that your Sex Offender Registration Law use ordinary words and not just legal terms to tell you what a person has been convicted of, so that you can understand it fully.
- Insist that it use words responsibly: calling a non-violent act 'violent' or a sex act committed without force as 'rape' just because there was a minor involved does not tell you what you are entitled to know.
- Tell your elected officials that you want judges left free to hand down sentences, instead of being tied to law books telling them what the sentence must be. Judges who are elected are elected to reflect your community's views. Make sure that they are left free to do so.

- Do not let your lawmakers interfere with a sex offender's healing by denying him a place to live and work.
- Ask your local lawmakers if such laws already exist and, if so, demand their immediate repeal. Recovering sex offenders who are not allowed to recover can only become repeat sex offenders.
- Do not let irresponsible members of the community force lawfully-registered sex offenders out of the community or they will return to living among you in secret once again.
- Remember that most sex offenders are not violent; their victim is usually someone they know; their method is usually deception and not physical brutality or force.
- Successful programs operated and run by volunteers have already succeeded in keeping convicted sex offenders from re-offending, and you and your friends and neighbors could start programs just like them in your community.
- When you find a convicted sex offender living near you, have the police tell you when that person completed their sentence, if they have had any problems since, whether they are now under supervision by parole or probation and, if so, the name and office telephone number of that community supervisor.
- Organize your neighbors to work with that supervisor so you can make certain that any sex offender living in your community stays in recovery.

To prevent tomorrow's sexual predator (Chapter 1)

Look for the sexually abused or emotionally battered child of today and befriend him or her, and you may save a life from turning in on itself and becoming destructive.

- If the child tells you that he or she has been physically or sexually abused, report it to police or Child Protective Services.
- If the child is being neglected, let the child know that he or she is welcome to visit you.

- Saving the nation from its next serial killer, rapist or child molester is simple. If you meet a child who is hungry, feed them. If you meet a child who is cold, give them a blanket. If you meet a child who doesn't have a shelter, become one for them. Don't wait until they grow up to become every parent's worst nightmare. Dare to comfort them now and involve your neighbors so that the child has a small community of adults who can be turned to for help. It takes a family to grow a child. It takes a community to heal one.

About The Author

Just before the new century began, the United States passed *Megan's Law*, requiring the registration of every convicted sex offender in the country and dissemination of their identity to the public. **Jake Goldenflame** was the first to openly champion it as one who fell under it. (See: "Advice from a registered sex offender," *San Francisco Examiner*, August 18,1997.)

That caught the eye of California's attorney general and, shortly thereafter, Jake began giving interviews to the media in conjunction with his state justice department's public information efforts. When Megan's Law later came before the United States Supreme Court for review, his story began to unfold nationally as *USA Today* wrote up his life, *People* magazine did a photo article on him and he became a featured guest on *The Oprah Winfrey Show,* which described his work in helping former victims to heal while encouraging sex offenders to accept this new law.

E-mail and letters began to pour into him from all over the world, asking questions that only a person like him could answer: *Why was I abused? How can I heal? How can I stop offending?* And, most importantly of all, *How can I protect my child?*

OVERCOMING SEXUAL TERRORISM is his answer, drawn from his own experiences, the sex offenders he has met in prison, therapists and members of law enforcement and community corrections. It answers every parent's worst nightmare by giving them steps they can take in their own home to make their neighborhood into a sheltering fortress that will protect its children.

Megan's Law soon began to evolve. Within three years of its passage, the version in Jake's state was amended over 200 ways, causing it to become so complex that a layman's version was needed. For this reason, in 2000, with the guidance of his state bar association, Jake published the first web site designed for those who fell under that law, writing openly as one of them. (www.calsexoffenders.net) He not only explained the law in the average person's terms, but included a list of recovery resources, available world-wide, that anyone could use who is struggling against sexual compulsions. Several years afterwards, aided by a public defender's office, he added a crisis counseling page for any sex offender who has become a fugitive, with instructions on how to safely surrender to law enforcement.

In 1998, Jake took the same first vows given to every Buddhist monk (*jukai*), plus a special one: to devote his life to helping anyone injured by sexual abuse. Immediately afterwards, he began a prison outreach project, encouraging incarcerated sex offenders to reach recovery. The year after that he conducted dialogue groups, as an admitted former sexual abuser, with former victims of sexual abuse at the International Forgiveness Conference held at the Findhorn Foundation, in the United Kingdom.

He subsequently participated in the Victim Offender Mediation Training Conference co-sponsored by the Texas Department of Criminal Justice and became a member of the Victim Offender Mediation Association, a restorative justice organization whose membership ranks include prosecutors, public defenders, corrections and law enforcement personnel, psychotherapists and counselors.

In 2002, Jake presented his website's "Ten Commandments for the Recovering Sex Offender" before the San Francisco Bay Area Treatment Network of the California Coalition on Sexual Offending and since then has been told of its use by sex offender therapists internationally.

Well over a half-century earlier, his life had begun in West Los Angeles, where he says that he was born and raised "with a bunch of movie studio brats." Almost all of his schoolmates had fathers who worked at the studios, in the sound department, special effects crews or as actors, directors or musical composers. He says that he even went steady briefly with a girl whose father won an Oscar. His last name is the English-language version of his family's original one, based upon their earlier occupation as goldsmiths.

He became a journalist in the U.S. Army, when he was trained to become a public information specialist. Several months later, he was the one who notified the press when remains of the Soviet Union's first space satellite, *Sputnik,* fell to earth near his army post in Alaska. "The story went global," he says. "I got phone calls from news organizations all over the world. That's pretty exciting stuff for a 20-year-old kid, handling his first major story."

Upon returning from active duty, he began studying at the University of Southern California School of Journalism, later receiving his B.A. in Social Sciences and then an M.A. in American Studies. He was hired as a newspaper reporter on a community weekly, later moving on to becoming a member of the public relations staff at a national charity organization and then a vacation substitute at a citywide newswire service.

To meet the rising costs of marriage and a family, he left print journalism for awhile. But in 1968 he began what became a ten-year stint as the West Coast contributing editor of a film magazine for entrants in the technical side of the motion picture industry. In 1970, he wrote a book on rising radical tensions in America, *Guerilla Warfare in the United States* (published by Weiss, Day and Lord, in Los Angeles).

In 1980 he began the study of law at Southwestern University School of Law in Los Angeles and received his doctorate from People's College of Law in 1985.

He has since become a tireless champion of recovery for all sex offenders and all former victims of sexual abuse and has now spoken on the subject of recovery before psychotherapists, sex offender therapy groups, victim recovery groups and an international conference. His work has been quoted by his state's handbook on Megan's Law under two attorneys-general in a row and he remains regularly featured by the media and listed on leading search engines, with articles about him appearing in numerous publications in the United States, Canada and England as well as television appearances on Cable and network channels plus interviews on radio stations throughout the English-speaking world and National Public Radio.

Seminars based upon this book are available and can be presented by Jake in your community or before your community organization. To request fees and terms, send an e-mail requesting Seminar Information to: goldenflame@sbcglobal.net or a letter addressed to:

Jake Goldenflame, J.D., M.A.

P.O. Box 424250

San Francisco, CA 94142-4250

Notes

Introduction: From Panic to Power

"Tough residency law spurs debate on sex offenders," *Los Angeles Times*, December 15, 2002

Lawrence A. Greenfeld, "Sex Offenses and Offenders: An Analysis of Data on Rape and Sexual Assault," U.S. Department of Justice, Office of Justice Programs, Bureau of Justice Statistics, February 1997, NCJ-163392, at: http://www.vaw.umn.edu/documents/sexoff/sexoff.html

Connecticut v. Doe,—U.S.—, 123 S.Ct. 1160, 155 L.Ed.2d 98 (2003)

"Meet the child molester next door," by Janet Kornblum, *USA TODAY* January 29, 2003, Life Section D p.1, col. 2

"Out of the Shadows," J.D. Heyman, Vickie Bane, *PEOPLE* 3/24/03, p. 121ff

Chapter 1 The Making of a Predator

Edith Hamilton, *Mythology.* (Boston, 1942)

Lucifer. www.lds-mormon.com/lucifer.shtml

Joseph D. McInerney, "GENES and BEHAVIOR, A complex relationship" in *Judicature* Genes and Justice, the Growing Impact of the New Genetics on the Courts, November-December 1999 Vol 83(3) at www.ornl.gov/hgmis/publicat/judicature/article4.html

Susan Forward, Ph.D., with Craig Buck, *TOXIC PARENTS Overcoming Their Hurtful Legacy and Reclaiming Your Life*, New York, 1989.

Chapter 2 The Theology of Sexuality

Edith Hamilton, *Mythology.* (Boston, 1942)

Robert Louis Stevenson, *Dr. Jekyll and Mr. Hyde.* (New York, 1981)

Chapter 3 Victims and Consequences

Susan Forward, Ph.D., with Craig Buck, *TOXIC PARENTS Overcoming Their Hurtful Legacy and Reclaiming Your Life*, (New York, 1989)

The I Ching or BOOK OF CHANGES. Richard Wilhelm, tr. Rendered into English by Cary F. Baynes. (Princeton, New Jersey, 1967)

Chapter 4 The Man with Nothing Left to Lose

G. Blanchard, "Aboriginal Canadian Innovations in the Treatment of Sexual Violence," *The Carnes Update*, Summer 1997, 4-6.

Rupert Ross, *Returning to the Teachings: Exploring Aboriginal Justice.* (New York, 1996.

Prabhavananda, S. & Isherwood,C., trs., *The Song of God: Bhagavad Gita*, New York, 1972)

The Story of Joseph: Genesis, Chapters 37-50.

Chapter 5 Evil or Ill?

Hanson, R.K., Gordon, A., Harris, A.J.R., Marques, J.K., Murphy, W., Quinsey, V.L., and Seto, M.C. (2002) First report of the Collaborative Outcome Data Project on the effectiveness of psychological treatment for sexual offenders. Sexual Abuse: A Journal of Research and Treatment, 14(2), 169-194

ALCOHOLICS ANONYMOUS, Third Edition. (New York, 1976)

J. K. Marques, C.L. Murrey and D.M. O'Connor, (1984). An innovative treatment program for sex offenders: Report to the Legislature. Sacramento: California Department of Mental Health.

Patrick J. Carnes, *Out of the Shadows: Understanding Sexual Addiction*, 2nd edition, (Center City, Minn., 1992)

Patrick J. Carnes, *HOPE AND RECOVERY A Twelve Step guide for healing from compulsive sexual behavior*, (Minnesota, 1987)

Anna C. Salter, *PREDATORS Pedophiles, Rapists and Other Sex Offenders*. (New York, 2003) pp. 82-87.

Comet, J., de Leval, F. and Mormont, C. (1999) Summary: Comparative Study: specialized and structured treatment of sex offenders in Europe. CRASC, rue de Merode 199, 1060, Bruxelles, Belgium.

Freddy Gazan, The Taking Charge of Sex Offenders in Each of the 15 Countries of the European Union: Legal and Therapeutic Perspectives. A presentation given at the 17th Annual Research and Treatment Conference of the Association for the Treatment of Sexual Abusers (ATSA) held in Vancouver, British Columbia, Canada October 14-17, 1998. Abstracts of ATSA. The Battle Without Borders: Confronting Sexual Abuse in Today's World.

Michel Foucault, *THE HISTORY OF SEXUALITY, VOLUME I An Introduction*. (New York, 1990)

McKune v. Lile, 153 L.Ed.II 47, 536 US—, 122 S.Ct.—(2002)

Kansas v. Hendricks, 521 U.S. 346, 117 S.Ct. 2072 (1997)

W.L. Marshall, D.R. Laws and H.E. Barbaree, *Handbook of Sexual Assault: Issues Theories and Treatment of the Offender*, (New York, 1990)

Vernon L. Quinsey and Christopher M. Earls, "The Modification of Sexual Preferences," Chapter 16, *Op.Cit.*

Sharon M. Williams & Murray C. Cullen, "Assessing and Treating Empathy Deficits in Sex Offenders: Melding Theory, Research and Practice," Abstracts of the 2000 Research and Treatment Conference of the American Association for the Treatment of Sexual Abusers

R. Karl Hanson, "Understanding the Relationship Between Empathy and Sexual Offending," Abstracts of the 1998 Research and Treatment Conference of the Association for the Treatment of Sexual Abusers

John Bergman, "Life, the Life Event, and Theater: A Personal Narrative on the Use of Drama Therapy with Sex Offenders," Chapter 17 in *THE SEX OFFENDER: Corrections, Treatment and Legal Practice, Vol. 1*, Schwartz, B.K. and Cellini, H.R., eds. Civic Research Institute, Inc. (1995)

John Nash, "Processing Problems and Neurotherapy: Differential Diagnosis and the Use of EEG Biofeedback with Adolescents and Adults, a paper presented at the 1998 Research and Treatment Conference of the Association for the Treatment of Sexual Abusers.

Chapter 6 Wrestling with the Sexual Self

T'rumath Tzvi: The Pentateuch. ("Hirsch Chumash") R. Ephraim Oratz, ed. Gertrude Hirschler, tr. (Booklyn, N.Y., 1986)

Webster's New World Hebrew Dictionary. Hayim Baltsan, ed. (New Jersey, 1992)

Gershom Scholem, *Major Trends in Jewish Mysticism.*(New York, 1974)

Louis Ginzberg, *Legends of the Jews.*(Philadelphia, 1956)

Ephod, See: *Ex. 28:4-40, 35:27* and *39:2-30* as well as the entry **Ephod** in *The Oxford Companion to the Bible.* Metzger and Coogan, eds. (New York, 1993(and *International Standard Bible Encyclopedia.* Bromiley, ed. (Michigan, 1982)

Brown, Driver and Briggs. *Hebrew-English Lexicon.* (Peabody, Mass.,1996)

The I Ching or BOOK OF CHANGES. Richard Wilhelm, tr. Rendered into English by Cary F. Baynes. (Princeton, New Jersey, 1967)

Aleksandr Solzhenitsyn, *The Gulag Archipelago 1918–1956 An Experiment in Literary Investigation I-II.* (New York,1973, 1974)

Elie Wiesel, *NIGHT.* (New York, 1960)

William Alexander, *Cool Water: Alcoholism, Mindfulness, and Ordinary Recovery,* Shambhala, (Boston & London, 1997)

John Bradshaw, *Bradshaw on: The Family* (Revised Edition). (Florida, 1996)

Pia Mellody, with A.W. Miller and J.K. Miller. *Facing Codependence.* (San Francisco, 1989)

Robert E. Freeman-Longo, "An Introduction to Relapse Prevention with Adolescent and Adult Sexual Abusers." A presentation given at the 1998 Research and Treatment Conference of the Association for the Treatment of Sexual Abusers and published in its *Abstracts* of that conference.

W.D. Pithers, and G.F. Cumming, "Relapse Prevention: A Method for Enhancing Behavioral Self-Management and External Supervision of the Sexual Aggressor," Chapter 20 in *The Sex Offender, Vol 1: Corrections, Treatment and Legal Practice.* Schwartz & Cellini, eds. New York: Civic Research Institute, 1995

Solicitor General Canada. *Triggers of Sexual Offense Recidivism*, Research Summary: Corrections Research and Development, Vol. 3 No. 4, July, 1998

William L. Shirer, *THE RISE AND FALL OF THE THIRD REICH: A History of Nazi Germany.* (New York, 1960) Pp. 322-323.

Sophocles, "King Oedipus," in *THE THEBAN PLAYS*, E.F. Watling, tr. (New York, 1947)

Homer, *The Iliad,* Robert Fagles, tr. New York, 1990

Chapter 7 Fate or Free Will

Fagles, Robert, tr., *Sophocles The Three Theban Plays*, (New York 1982)

Fagles, Robert, tr., *Homer The Iliad*, (New York, 1990)

Chapter 8 The Myth of Self

The Essential Rumi. Coleman Barks, tr. with John Moyne, A.J. Arberry and Reynold Nicholson. (San Francisco, 1995)

Chapter 9 Sex Offender in the Community

Kathy Evans, "The Crime Society Can't Forgive." *Sunday Age* (Australia) 29 August 1999

Kathleen Ingley, "Scholar Suggests City of Molesters." *The Arizona Republic* May 2, 1999

Anne Rice, *Interview with the Vampire: A Novel,* New York: 1976

Fred S. Berlin, "Issues in the Exploration of Biological Factors Contributing to the Etiology of the 'Sex offender,' plus Some Ethical Considerations," 528 Annals of the New York Academy of Sciences (1988) at 183-192

The Oprah Winfrey Show, February 25, 2003

Aesop's Fables, Online Collection at: http://www.pacificnet.net/~johnr/aesop/

W.L. Marshall, et.al, "Treatment Outcome with Sexual Offenders," *Clinical Psychology Review*, Vol. 11, pp. 465-485, 1991

Marques, et. al, "The Sex Offender Treatment and Evaluation Project, Fourth Report to the Legislature in Response to PC 1365," Division of State Hospitals, Department of Mental Health, October, 1991, p. 5

Sheila A. Campbell, Battling Sex Offenders: Is Megan's Law An Effective Means of Achieving Public Safety? Seton Hall Legislative Journal, Vol. 19, pp. 519-563, 1995

Tracy L. Silva, Dial '1-900-PERVERT" and Other Statutory Measures That Provide Public Notification of Sex Offenders. Southern Methodist University Law Review, Vol. 48, No. 4, May-Jun 1995, pp. 1961-1994

Dean E. Murphy, "Justice as a Morality Play That Ends with Shame." The New York Times on the Web for June 3, 2001.

Jake Goldenflame, "Advice from a Registered Sex Offender." *San Francisco Examiner*, August 18, 1997, A-15

Nathaniel Hawthorne, *"THE SCARLET LETTER," in* FOUR CLASSIC AMERICAN NOVELS, (New York, 1969)

Child Protection (Offenders Registration) Act 2000-SECT 10, New South Wales Consolidated Acts, http://www.austlii.edu.au/au/legis/nsw/consol_act/cpra2000403/

Queensland (Australia) Criminal Law Amendment Act 1945 Office of the Queensland Parliamentary Counsel

Sex Offender Registry Act (British Columbia, Canada) http://www.legis.gov.bc.ca/2001/3rd_read/gov11-3.htm

Bill 31 1999 "Christopher's Act" (Ontario Province, Canada)

Sex Offenders Act, 2001 (Ireland)

Reuters, "Korea Puts Sex Offenders Online," 6:16 a.m., Aug. 30, 2001 PDT http://www.wired.com/news/print/0,1294,46437,00.html

Scottish Executive, The Sex Offenders Act 1997 Guidance for Agencies

Sex Offenders Act 1997 (for England, Wales, Northern Ireland and Scotland) HOC 39/1997

Home Office (U.K.), "New Clauses added to the Criminal Justice and Court Services Bill at Lords Committee" ('Sarah's Law'), a bulletin issued by Home Office (U.K.) 19 October 2000

Author's Web site for fellow offenders: www.calsexoffenders.net (See: Foreign Travel Advisory on Home Page)

Pamela Podger and Manny Fernandez, "Santa Rosa Sex Offender Found Dead: Suicide is suspected after Megan's law alert," in *San Francisco Chronicle*, July 7, 1998, www.sfgate.com

Kan Kikuchi, *Beyond the Pale of Vengeance*. Rev. Jisho Perry and Kimiko Vago, trs. (Mt Shasta, California: 1998).

Chapter 10 Establishing a Neighborhood Defense

W.L. Marshall, D.R. Laws and H.E. Barbaree, *Handbook of Sexual Assault: Issues, Theories and Treatment of the Offender,* (New York: 1990) p. 122

Randy Thornhill and Craig T. Palmer, *A NATURAL HISTORY OF RAPE: Biological Bases of Sexual Coercion,* (Cambridge: 2000, p. 77

Anna C. Salter, *PREDATORS PEDOPHILES, RAPISTS, AND OTHER SEX OFFENDERS,* (New York 2003)

Connecticut v. Doe,—U.S.—, 123 S.Ct. 1160, 155 L.Ed.2d 98 (2003)

KlaasKids Foundation "Sex offender and community notification for Alaska" www.klaaskids.orgs

Kansas v. Hendricks, 521 US 346, 117 S.Ct. 072 (1997) Dissenting Opinion by Justice Breyer

S.A. Johnson and A. Listiak, "The Measurement of Sexual Preferences—A Preliminary Comparison of Phallometry and the Abel Assessment," Chapter 26 in THE SEX OFFENDER, Schwartz, B.K. and Cellini, H.R., eds. Civic Research Institute, Kingston, New Jersey.

Gordon S. Wood, *The Creation of the American Republic 1776-1787* (Chapel Hill: 1998)

Elvia Diaz, "State laws sought on renting to sex convicts," *The Arizona Republic* Dec. 20,2002

Associated Press, January 7, 2003, "Governor wants to fire sex offender from state job," www.kobtv.com/archive

Kate Nash, "Mayor's bill would force sex convicts to say more," *Albuquerque Tribune* February 12, 2002

Kris Sherman, "Young sex offenders challenge schools," *The (Tacoma) News Tribune,* Tribnet.com, January 13, 2003

Todd S. Frankl, "School board to track sex offender students," *HeraldNet,* January 23, 2003

Jamie Swift," Tracking sex offenders by GPS," *Eastside Journal,* Ejonline, eastsidejournal.com, January 11, 2003

Marc Chase, "Senator reconsiders sex-offender housing restrictions," *Quad-City Times* (Iowa), www.qctimes.com

"Tough residency law spurs debate on sex offenders," *Los Angeles Times,* December 15, 2002

Illinois Criminal Code Sec. 11-9.3 Presence within school zone by child sex offenders prohibited

Chris Norwood, "Talladegans named in sex offenders' suit," *Alabama Daily Home,* March 2, 2003, www.dailyhome.com/news

Denise Sinclair, "Attorney general: Crimes against children must not be tolerated," *Alabama Daily Home,* April 25, 2003, www.dailyhome.com/news

House Bill 1011, State of Arkansas 84th General Assembly, Regular Sessions, 2003

Georgia General Assembly SB 101, www.legis.state.ga.us/legis/2003_04/sum/sb101.htm

First Regular Session House Bill Number. 84, 92nd General Assembly, State of Missouri, www.house.stat.mo.us/bills03/biltxt/intro/HB0084I.htm

State of Oklahoma, Engrossed House Bill No. 1501 by Cox and Monson

Bill Information for HB0865 and SB0740, State of Tennessee, www.legislature.state.tn.us/bills/currentga/BillCompanionInfo.asp

S.K. Bardwell, "Sex offenders clustering in poor neighborhoods," *Houston Chronicle,* January 25, 2003, HoustonChronicle.com

Richard Willing, "Laws tighten on sex offenders," *USA TODAY,* May 12, 2003

Chapter 11 How to Prevent Tomorrow's Crimes

Community-Based Sex Offender Program Evaluation Project Report to the Legislature (1999), St. Paul: Minnesota Department of Corrections.

Amicus Brief, Association for the Treatment of Sexual Abusers, *Connecticut v. Doe* No. 01-1231 in the Supreme Court of the United States (2003).)

Anna C. Salter, *PREDATORS: Pedophiles, Rapists and Other Sex Offenders* (New York, 2003). P. 97.

Community Reintegration Project Circles of Support & Accountability, Revised edition. E. Heise, L.Home, H. Kirkegaard, H. Night, I.P. Derry and M. Yantzi, eds. Toronto: Mennonite Central Committee Ontario under contract with Correctional Services Canada, 2000.

Evan Heinse and Richard Ratzlaff, "'Circles of Support' for Sex Offenders Include Victims," The Crime Victims Report, July/August 1997 at mcccos@web.net

Candis McLean, "Next step—a national registry," Report Newsmagazine, June 3, 2002, Alberta, Canada.

Neuces County Sheriff's Department, Corpus Christi, Texas

Government of Japan Ministry of Justice Research and Training Institute Summary of The White Paper on Crime 1997

Jill Tucker, "Giving treatment to child molesters," *San Mateo County Times Online* January 21, 2003. www.sanmateocountytimes.com

Reader's Resources

Note: All services described below are listed for information-only, no liability is assumed by the author for their use.

Books

Alexander, William, *Cool Water: Alcoholism, Mindfulness, and Ordinary Recovery,* Shambhala, (Boston & London 1997)

Baumeister, Roy F., EVIL: *Inside Human Violence and Cruelty,* W.E. Freeman and Company,(New York 1997, 1999)

Bradshaw, John, Homecoming: *Reclaiming and Championing Your Inner Child* (New York 1990)

Bradshaw, John, *BRADSHAW ON: THE FAMILY,* Health Communications Inc., 1996

CALIFORNIA's Megan's Law The First Year: Lifting the Shroud of Secrecy, California Department of Justice, May 1998.

Campbell, Joseph, *THE HERO WITH A THOUSAND FACES,* Third Princeton/Bollingen Paperback Printing, (Princeton, 1973)

Carnes, Patrick J., *OUT OF THE SHADOWS Understanding Sexual Addiction,* 2nd Edition, Hazelden Information and Educational Services, 1992

Carnes, Patrick J., *HOPE AND RECOVERY A Twelve Step guide for healing from compulsive sexual behavior,* Hazelden Information and Educational Services, 1987

Carnes, Patrick J., *HOPE AND RECOVERY The Workbook,* Hazelden Information and Educational Services, 1990

Forward, Susan, *TOXIC PARENTS: Overcoming Their Hurtful Legacy and Reclaiming Your Life,* (New York,1989) trade paperback January 2002

Foucault, Michel, *DISCIPLINE & PUNISH The Birth of the Prison*, Alan Sheridan tr., (New York 1995)

Hawthorne, Nathaniel, *THE SCARLET LETTER* in FOUR CLASSIC AMERICAN NOVELS, (New York 1969)

Homer, *THE ILIAD*, Robert Fagles, tr., (New York 1990)

Kikuchi, Kan, *Beyond the Pale of Vengeance*, tr. Rev. Jisho Perry and Kimiko Vago, (Mt. Shasta, California, 1998)

Mellody, Pia, et. al., *FACING CODEPENDENCE Where It comes From, How It Sabotages Our Lives*, (San Francisco, 1989)

Mellody, Pia, et. al, *BREAKING FREE: A Recovery Workbook for FACING CODEPENDENCE*, (San Francisco, 1989)

Morrison, Toni, *The Bluest Eye*, (New York, 1994)

Prabhavananda, S. & Isherwood,C., trs., *The Song of God: Bhagavad Gita*, (New York, 1972)

Ross, Rupert, *RETURNING TO THE TEACHINGS Exploring Aboriginal Justice*, (Canada, 1996)

Salter, Anna C., *PREDATORS: Pedophiles, Rapists, and Other Sex Offenders*, (New York, 2003)

Solzhenitsyn, Aleksandr I., *THE GULAG ARCHIPELAGO 1918–1956 An Experiment in Literary Investigation I–II*, Thomas P. Whitney, tr., (New York 1973)

Sophocles, "King Oedipus," in *SOPHOCLES THE THEBAN PLAYS*, E.F. Watling, tr., (New York, 1947)

Stevenson, Robert Louis, *Dr. Jekyll and Mr. Hyde*, (New York, 1985)

Thornhill, Randy and Palmer, Craig T., *A NATURAL HISTORYOF RAPE: Biological Bases of Sexual Coercion*, (Cambridge and London, 2000)

Elie Wiesel, *NIGHT.* (New York, 1960)

Wood, Gordon S., *THE CREATION OF THE AMERICAN REPUBLIC 1776-1787* (Chapel Hill: 1998)

Yantzi, Mark, *SEXUAL OFFENDING AND RESTORATION*, (Waterloo, Ontario, 1998)

Zukav, Gary, *The Seat of the Soul*, (New York, 1989)

Journals

PROFESSIONAL COUNSELOR: Serving the Addictions and Mental Health Fields
Health Communications Inc., 3201 Southwest 15th Street, Deerfield Beach, FL 33442-8190
Website: www.professionalcounselor.com
Subscriber Services: P.O. Box 420235, Palm Coast, FL 32142-0235
Tele. (800) 998-0793

SEXUAL ADDICTION & COMPULSIVITY: The Journal of Treatment and Prevention
(Adapted as The Journal of the National Council on Sexual Addiction and Compulsivity)
Patrick J. Carnes, Ph.D., Editor in Chief
Website: www.tandfdc.com/jnls/sac.htm#top
Subscription Services:
Taylor & Francis Order Dept.
47 Runway Road, Suite "G"
Levittown, PA 19057-4000
Tele. (800) 821-8312

Websites

Circles of Support and Accountability (Mennonite)
#6 Trinity Square, third floor
Toronto, Ontario M5G 1B1

Tele. 416 596 9341

A community reintegration project sponsored by the Mennonite Community to assist convicted sex offenders being released from prison with reintegrating themselves into society while remaining self-controlled. Presently operates primarily in Ontario province but willing to assist other communities elsewhere in creating similar projects they can operate themselves through their own faith-based organizations.

American Foundation for Addiction Research
Links to Web Resources in the field of addictions.
Website: www.addiction/research.com/

"How Do I Know if I Am A Sex Addict?" an article by Robert Weiss, LCSW, CAS, Clinical Director, The Sexual Recovery Institute, Los Angeles, Orange County. Website: www.sexualrecovery.com

Sex Addiction Screening Test of 25 questions with self-scoring guide to determine whether there are issues of sexual addiction requiring exploration with a professional clinician; link to list of clinics, therapists, publishers and some 12 Step Groups. (Online resource of Patrick J. Carnes, Ph.D., editor of Sexual Addiction & Compulsivity)
Website: www.sexhelp.com

The National Council on Sexual Compulsivity And Compulsivity
Provides research, newsletters, journals, conferences, support in reducing stigma of sexual addiction, sexual compulsivity and sexual offending
1090 Northchase Parkway Suite 200 South, Marrietta, GA 30067
Tele. Area Code (770) 989-9754
Website: www.ncsac.org

California Coalition on Sexual Offending
5361 N. Pershing Ave., Ste. H
Stockton, CA 95207
www.ccoso.org

Coalition members are representatives from law enforcement, criminal justice, mental health, probation, parole and community services dedicated to addressing the issues related to sexual offending. Regional chapters meet regularly to allow members to network and exchange approaches and discoveries that may aid in reducing recidivism among both youthful and adult perpetrators of sexual crimes.

SATA-SORT

Sex Abuse Treatment Alliance promotes education and political action through its program on behalf of everyone affected by sexual abuse. Publishes newsletter, SATA-SORT News, four times a year, with contributions from offenders in custody and others. Also website at: www.satasort.org For more information, write:

SATA-SORT News
P.O. Box 1191
Okemos, MI 48805-1191

Victim Offender Mediation Association (VOMA)
Claire Harris, Administrator
2233 University Ave W, Suite 300
St Paul MN 55114
Tele.(612) 874-0570
FAX 651-644-4227
E-mail: voma@voma.org
VOMA Web Site

Center for Restorative Justice & Peacemaking
University of Minnesota
School of Social Work
1404 Gortner Ave, 105 Peters Hall
St. Paul MN 55108-6160

Tele. (612) 624-4923
FAX (612) 625-8224
E-mail: rjp@tlcmail.che.umn.edu
Website

PRISON FAMILIES ANONYMOUS

A support system for families who now have or ever had a loved one involved in the juvenile or criminal justice system. Support group meetings available.

For more information, write:
Prison Families Anonymous

45 Prairie Drive,
N. Babylon, NY 11703
or E-mail: allanpfa@optonline.net

The National Association of Attorneys General
News, Issues, Research and list of all attorneys general in the states and territories of the United States. Drop-down menu takes readers to a page listing their state's attorney general along with that office's phone number, address and own website.
Website: www.naag.org/

www.calsexoffenders.net
The recovering sex offender's website. An introduction to the sex offender registration law, guidance in how to earn one's way back as a registered sex offender, crisis counseling suggestions and list of recovery resources worldwide for those suffering from sexual compulsions. E-mail link to author.

Professional Referral Organizations

Association for the Treatment of Sexual Abusers (ATSA)
4900 SW Griffith Drive, Suite 274
Beaverton, Oregon 97005

Makes referrals to qualified psychotherapists, clinicians and other professionals among its members throughout the United States and abroad who adhere to its ethical standards and provide recognized treatment to sex offenders.

Tele. (503) 643-1023
ATSA Website
E-mail: atsa@atsa.com

The Safer Society Foundation
P.O. Box 340
Brandon, Vt. 05733-0340
Tele. (802) 247-5141
Monday thru Fridays
9:00 A.M. to 5:00 P.M. E.T.
A nonprofit agency for the prevention and treatment of sexual abuse that also offers referrals to therapists for those requesting the same.
Web Site

Stop It Now!
P.O. Box 495
Haydenville, MA 01039
Tele. (888) 773-8368
Web Site
runs a toll-free confidential helpline open five days a week, 9 to 5, offering information and referrals to those requesting the same

Sexual Abuse Treatment Program (SATP) Canada
39 Stirling Ave., N.
Kitchener, ON N2H 3G4

Offender Program and Survivor Program. Educational Groups, Process Groups, Partners Program, Referrals, Speakers Bureau. Special program available for federally sentenced women helps with reintegrating them into their communities across Ontario.

Tele. (519) 744-6549
Fax (519) 744-2172
Email: cjiwr@cjiwr.com
WEBSITE: www.cjiwr.com

National Adolescent Perpetration Network
Kempe Children's Center
University of Colorado Health Sciences Center
1825 Marion
Denver, Colorado 80218

A cooperative network of professionals working with sexually abusive youth in the United States and abroad. Facilitates communication among those treating children and adolescents who are at risk of becoming chronic sex offenders. Provides information and referrals upon request.

Tele. (303) 864-5252
FAX (303) 864-5179
E-mail: ryan.gail@tchden.org
Web site: NAPN

Self Recovery Organizations

At least eight organizations exist in the United States, some with branches abroad, that use an approach based upon the Twelve Step program of Alcoholics Anonymous to handle sexual addictions. Their members vary from those whose compulsions are no more than "social nuisances," such as exhibitionism, to others who are addicted to compulsive phone sex, extramarital relationships, promiscuous relationships in public places, and worse (although most members I met have never been convicted of a felony).

Using the language of alcoholism and drug addiction counseling, they vary among themselves as to what constitutes "sexual sobriety," or addictive-free behavior, ranging from 'no sex of any kind, other than with one's marital spouse' to 'avoiding whatever each person feels is addictive.' Open to men—and women—ready to stop engaging in compulsive self-destructive sexual behavior and (in the case of four of these organizations) to the spouses, relatives or friends of sex addicts—they offer self-help manuals and literature, regular meetings for group support, and one-on-one encouragement by more experienced members plus, in many instances, a local network of members who can be called upon for help whenever it's needed.

Sexaholics Anonymous
Post Office Box 111910
Nashville, TN 37222
Tele. (615) 331-6230
Email: saico@sa.org

Formed in 1976, Sexaholics Anonymous offers help to those who have lost control and are "addicted to lust." Holding the most demanding standard among these organizations, SA defines destructive sexual behavior as *any form of sex with one's self or with partners other than the spouse*, and for the unmarried, *any form of sex*.

They condemn *lust* even with a marital partner, in masturbation or in sex in dreams.

Their program begins by requiring an admission from the new participant of being a prisoner to "a power greater than ourselves," even though each individual is also urged to see their self as being that power's active agent. (From *Sexaholics Anonymous*, 1989)

Support is given through group meetings, one-to-one counseling by a more experienced sponsor-member selected by the new member, and literature containing lessons learned by others plus the Twelve Steps of Alcoholics Anonymous as applied to sexual compulsion.

Each member is urged to:
    make a totally-honest self-inventory;
    give up the right to live a self-damaging life;
    pray for help to God, as each person defines that word;
    make amends whenever possible to anyone harmed, and to
    forgive those who have harmed the member.

Sexaholics Anonymous is not affiliated with any religious denomination. In its 1989 book, *Member Stories*, accounts are furnished by twenty members—who had belonged for at least three years at the time of their writing—as to what living as a sex addict was like, what made them change and what it is like to be in recovery, ranging from a woman—whose addiction drove her into prostitution and "almost incest" before discovering Sexaholics Anonymous—to a closet homosexual, a child molester, an ex-priest and others.

In its 1982 pamphlet entitled *Sexaholics Anonymous*, the disconnection from the rest of life that a sex addict feels, the intrigue he or she courts for thrills, and the overwhelming shame that follows are accurately reported. A twenty question checklist is included along with a statement of known results possible for anyone who wants to change that kind of life.

With branches in the United States and abroad, literature and a newsletter, and a Corrections Committee that works with prisoners, Sexaholics Anonymous charges no dues or fees at any of its meetings and respects the confidentiality of those who attend.

S-Anon International Family Groups
Post Office Box 11242
Nashville, TN 37222-1242
Tele. (615) 833-3152
FAX (615) 331-6901

As an adjunct to Sexaholics Anonymous, SAnon International Family Groups provides support and Twelve Step training to families and friends of sexual addicts, maintaining that no one but the addict can control the addict's behavior and urging others not to unfairly blame themselves for what the addict does. The emphasis is on helping those who are close to the addict recover themselves. Literature, in either English or Spanish, is available at nominal prices. Branch locations available upon request.

Sex Addicts Anonymous
Post Office Box 70949
Houston, TX 77270
Tele. (713) 869-4902
Tele. (713) 869-4902
Email: info@saa-recovery.org
Formed in 1994, Sex Addicts Anonymous is a self-help organization open to men and women who share a desire to stop engaging in compulsive sexual behavior. They urge abstinence not from all sexual activity outside of marriage, like Sexaholics Anonymous, but only from the kinds that *each member individually finds compulsive and destructive for them*, a far more liberal standard.

No dues or fees. Helpful literature is available at nominal prices, including the pamphlet *Getting Started in Sex Addicts Anonymous*, which includes a twelve-question self-assessment and a list of tips on how to cope with situations where one doesn't want to act-out, ranging from indecent exposure to engaging in prostitution to engaging in child sexual abuse.

Now located in various communities in the United States and in Puerto Rico, the organization also claims branches in eleven countries including: Argentina, Australia, Canada, People's Republic of China (Hong Kong); United Kingdom; Finland, Germany, India, Mexico, Uruguay and Panama.

The organization also works with prisoners by sending them self-help literature that includes how any of them may start a group with the assistance of a prison sponsor.

Sex and Love Addicts Anonymous
Post Office Box 650010
West Newton, MA 02165-0010
Tele. (617) 332-1845
E-mail: SLAAfws@aol.com

Begun in Boston, in 1976, as The Augustine Fellowship—to avoid contro-versy—Sex and Love Addicts Anonymous occupies the middle ground between the standards of the other two major groups for compulsives by defining sexual sobriety as not engaging in *any sexual activity except "that which would be worked out in a committed, continuing relationship"*, and where none exists, calling for a period of sexual abstinence. Hence, under this organization's standards, one need not be lawfully married to their partner in order to live a sexually sober life.

Addictive behavior includes any sexual activity *or emotional relationship* that is out of control and threatens to destroy the rest of the person's life. It is, therefore, both for those with problems with a sexual addiction or an obsessive emotional attachment.

Recovering Couples Anonymous
Post Office Box 11872
St. Louis, Missouri 63105
Tele. (314) 397-0867, (314) 830-2600
FAX (314) 397-1319, (314) 830-2670
Website: http://www.recovering-couples.org

To rebuild the marital or partnership relationship damaged by sexual addiction, Recovering Couples Anonymous (RCA) was founded in the late 1980's for couples seeking a sense of intimacy outside of addiction or co-addiction to drinking, sexual compulsivity and/or co-dependency. Employing the Twelve Step program, parenting contracts and "fighting" contracts for couples, they hold meetings in some eighty locations in approximately twenty-five states; Canada, England, Sweden, Trinidad and Tobago. A checklist of characteristics of functional and dysfunctional cou-ples, a newsletter, literature and an audiotape price list, is available, plus location of the nearest meeting. No dues or fees are charged to attend meetings.

Sexual Recovery Anonymous
Post Office Box 72044
4429 Kingway
Burnaby, B.C.,
VSH 4P9, Canada
Tele. (604) 290-93872

Post Office Box 73
New York, NY 10024
Tele (212) 340-4650
Website: www/ourworld.compuserve.com/homepages/sra

Another organization that offers assistance to couples *or* singles where sobriety is defined as not engaging in any sexual activities outside of a mutually committed relationship. SRA offers a twelve-step program based on Alcoholics Anonymous at any of twenty-four meetings weekly in the states of New York, New Jersey and Connecticut.

COSA (Partners)
9337-B Katy Freeway
Suite 142
Houston, TX 77024
Tele. (612) 537-6904

Dedicated to helping partners of sexual addicts, Co-Sex Addicts (Co-SA) also offers a twelve step program. For more information, contact them through the phone number and address listed above.

Sexual Compulsives Anonymous
Post Office Box 1585
Old Chelsea Station
New York, NY 10011
Tele. (800) 977-HEAL
(212) 606-3778 (New York City & International)
Website: www.SCA-Recovery.Org

Active both in New York and San Francisco, SCA offers a twelve-step program for men and women who wish to overcome engaging in sexually compulsive behavior by adopting a more responsible set of sexual boundaries.

Is participation in any group really necessary?

"No one who has turned his back on addiction has lasted long without 'community'…We are co-dependent…nothing can exist alone."
  - William Alexander, *Cool Water: Alcoholism, Mindfulness, and Ordinary Recovery*, Shambhala Publications, 1997

United Nations Convention on the Rights of the Child

In 1989 The United Nations unanimously adopted The Convention on the Rights of the Child. It went into force in 1990, seven months later, after the twentieth State had ratified it. Since then it has been ratified by all States with the exception of Somalia, which had no government at the time, and the United States. It has four general principles:
  - Children must not suffer discrimination regardless of their race, color, sex, language, religion, political or other opinion, national, ethnic or social origin, property, disability, birth or other status;
  - Children have a right to survival and development in all aspects of their lives, including the physical, emotional, psycho-social, cognitive, social and cultural;
  - The best interests of the child must be a primary consideration in all decisions or actions that affect the child or children as a group; whether these decisions are made by governmental, administrative or judicial authorities, or by families themselves, and
  - Children must be allowed as active participants in all matters affecting their lives and be free to express their opinions, have their views heard and taken seriously.

As UNICEF points out, in many societies children are seen only as their parents' property, or as adults in the making or as not yet ready to contribute to society. This landmark treaty places the care and protection of every person under 18 years of age—every child—as a priority for everyone, especially for governments. The Convention has established new ethical principals and international norms of behavior towards children.

It is comprehensive, the only one to ensure children their civil, political, economic, social and cultural rights;

It is universal, applying to all children in all situations in virtually the entire community of nations.

It is unconditional, calling on even those governments with scarce resources to take action to protect children's rights, and

The Convention is holistic, asserting that all rights are essential, indivisible, interdependent and equal.

Under the Convention, every child has a right to live with his or her parents or maintain contact if separated from either one; cross national borders to be reunified with his or her parents, and be protected from abuse and neglect by parents or care givers.

Every child has the right to special protection in situations of exploitation such as child labor, drug abuse, sexual exploitation or sexual abuse, sale, trafficking and abduction.

Every child has the right to a name and nationality; protection from being deprived of his or her identity; freedom of expression; freedom of thought, conscience and religion; freedom of association and peaceful assembly; information from a diversity of sources; privacy; protection from torture or other cruel, inhuman or degrading treatment or punishment, and protection against unlawful arrest and unjustified deprivation of liberty.

Every child under the age of 18 years is protected from being punished by death or imprisonment for life without the possibility of release.

There are six Articles in particular which impact sexual offenders.

Under Article 34 of the Convention, States are to protect the child from all forms of sexual exploitation and sexual abuse, and particularly are required to take all national, bilateral and multilateral measures to prevent the inducement or coercion of a child to engage in any unlawful sexual activity; the exploitative use of children in prostitution or other unlawful sexual practices, and the exploitative use of children in pornographic performances and materials.

Under Article 19, States are required to protect the child from all forms of physical or mental violence, injury or abuse, including sexual abuse, while in the care of parents, legal guardians or any other person who has the care of the child.

Under Article 32, States shall protect the child from economic exploitation and from performing any work likely to be harmful to the child's mental, spiritual, moral or social development.

Under Article 35, States shall take all multilateral measures to prevent the abduction, sale or traffic in children for any purpose whatsoever.

Under Article 36, States shall protect the child from all other forms of exploitation prejudicial to any aspects of the child's welfare.

Under Article 39, States shall take all appropriate measures to promote psychological recovery and social reintegration of a child victim of any form of exploitation or abuse and do so in an environment fostering the health, self-respect and dignity of the child.

States having endorsed the Convention are accountable for ensuring that the human rights of children are realized, and their progress is monitored by the UN Committee on the Rights of the Child, an internationally elected body of ten independent experts with experience and expertise in children's rights. Countries must report to the Committee two years after ratifying the Convention and every five years thereafter.

Since the providing of therapeutic treatment to convicted sex offenders now has a demonstrable record of reducing further sexual exploitation of children, it may be appropriate for the implementing body of this Convention to encourage wider development and application of the same within more nations of the world.

UNICEF, The Convention on the Rights of the Child

Index

use of methods similar to Alcoholic Anonymous, 95
vow to help victims, 131
website for fellow registrants, 132
writing, 118, 121, 134

Suicide, 8, 38, 71
county jail, 47-49, 53, 55
Gay section of jail, 50
daily routines, 51
protective housing in,49
sex in, 50
violence in, 51

Teen Prostitution, 17
boy prostitutes, 27-32, 115, 126-127
Children of the Night, 32, 169
jail and, 30
preventing, ending, 32
violence and, 30

Treatment, therapies
aversive conditioning, 107
answers regarding parental factors, 82-83
anti-addiction counseling, 94-99
barriers to, 35
community, 165
community service as part of, 150
control, not 'cure,' 66-67
cry for help, 22, 39
earlier methods, 65-66
failure of punishment alone, 67
fear of, 22
fear of own compulsivity, 80
for child sexual abuse victims, 15-16
for incest victim, 36-37
for perpetrator, 38

0-595-34210-8

Printed in the United States
38658LVS00006B/84

9 780595 342105